Emotional Intelligence: Your Ultimate Hands-On Guide

Mastering Self-Awareness, Empathy, and Relationships

© **Copyright 2024 - All rights reserved.**

The content contained within this book may not be reproduced, duplicated or transmitted without direct written permission from the author or the publisher.

Under no circumstances will any blame or legal responsibility be held against the publisher, or author, for any damages, reparation, or monetary loss due to the information contained within this book, either directly or indirectly.

Legal Notice:

This book is copyright protected. It is only for personal use. You cannot amend, distribute, sell, use, quote or paraphrase any part, or the content within this book, without the consent of the author or publisher.

Disclaimer Notice:

Please note the information contained within this document is for educational and entertainment purposes only. All effort has been executed to present accurate, up to date, reliable, complete information. No warranties of any kind are declared or implied. Readers acknowledge that the author is not engaged in the rendering of legal, financial, medical or professional advice. The content within this book has been derived from various sources. Please consult a licensed professional before attempting any techniques outlined in this book.

By reading this document, the reader agrees that under no circumstances is the author responsible for any losses, direct or indirect, that are incurred as a result of the use of the information contained within this document, including, but not limited to, errors, omissions, or inaccuracies.

Table of Contents

INTRODUCTION 1

CHAPTER 1: EMOTIONAL INTELLIGENCE 101 5

   ORIGINS OF EMOTIONAL INTELLIGENCE 6
      Self-Awareness 7
      Self-Regulation 8
      Empathy 8
      Social Skills 9
      Motivation 10
   DEBUNKING COMMON MYTHS 13
      Myth 1: EI Is the Same as IQ 13
      Myth 2: You Are Either Born With EI, or You Are Not 14
      Myth 3: EI Is All About Being Nice and Empathetic 14
      Myth 4: High EI Means You Never Experience Negative Emotions 15
      Myth 5: EI Is Only Useful in Personal Relationships 15
   QUICK SELF-ASSESSMENT QUIZ 16
      Quiz Instructions 16
      Scoring: 17
   REFLECTION QUESTIONS: UNDERSTANDING EMOTIONAL INTELLIGENCE 18

CHAPTER 2: THE SCIENCE BEHIND EMOTIONS 25

   MORE THAN FEELINGS 26
      The Brain's Role in Emotions 27
      The Difference Between IQ and EI 30
      How Are IQ and EI Measured? 31
      Can You Improve Your IQ and EI? 33
      Practical Applications of Emotional Science 34
   REFLECTION QUESTIONS 36

CHAPTER 3: SELF-AWARENESS: KNOW THYSELF 39

   MIRROR WITHIN 40
      Self-Reflection Matters 41
      Practical Tips for Effective Self-Reflection 42
      Identifying Emotional Triggers 43
      Managing Emotional Triggers 44
   TOOLS FOR BUILDING SELF-AWARENESS 45
      Journaling 45

- *Mindfulness* *46*
- *Feedback* *48*
- FURTHER RESOURCES 48
  - *Recommended Books* *48*
  - *Recommended Articles* *49*

CHAPTER 4: THE ART OF SELF-CONTROL 51

- MASTERING THE PAUSE 52
- SELF-CONTROL: IMPORTANCE IN DAILY LIFE 53
  - *Self-Control, Stress, and Anxiety* *53*
  - *Understanding Stress and Anxiety* *54*
  - *Stress and Anxiety Management Techniques* *57*
  - *Recognizing and Understanding Your Emotional Triggers* *59*
  - *Overcoming Procrastination* *61*
- EXERCISE: SELF-CONTROL DEVELOPMENT 62
  - *Step 1: Identify Your Triggers* *63*
  - *Step 2: Set Clear Goals* *63*
  - *Step 3: Develop Strategies* *63*
  - *Step 4: Implement the Strategies* *64*
  - *Step 5: Reflect and Analyze* *64*
  - *Step 6: Celebrate your Progress* *65*
  - *Step 7: Seek Support* *65*
  - *Additional Tips* *65*
- INTERACTIVE ELEMENT: STRESS MANAGEMENT EXERCISE 66
  - *Guided Exercise: Identifying Stress Triggers and Creating a Personalized Stress Management Plan* *66*
- REFLECTION QUESTIONS 68

CHAPTER 5: BUILDING RESILIENCE 73

- RESILIENCE MATTERS 75
- GROWTH MINDSET VERSUS A FIXED MINDSET 76
  - *Maintaining Emotional Balance* *79*
- FURTHER RESOURCES: RECOMMENDED BOOKS AND ARTICLES ON RESILIENCE 83
  - *Books* *84*
  - *Articles* *84*

CHAPTER 6: MOTIVATION AND GOAL SETTING 85

- THE CONNECTION BETWEEN EMOTIONAL INTELLIGENCE, MOTIVATIONS, AND YOUR GOALS 86
  - *Understanding Your Motivations* *86*
  - *Setting Goals With Emotional Awareness* *87*
  - *Managing Your Emotions on the Path to Goals* *87*
  - *Self-Motivation and Emotional Regulation* *87*
- IDENTIFYING YOUR MOTIVATIONS: UNDERSTANDING YOUR "WHY" 88

- Discovering Your Motivations and Goals 89
- Motivation Mapping Exercise 92
- Avoiding Common Pitfalls 94
- THE PATH TO SUCCESS: STAYING MOTIVATED 95
- EMOTIONAL INTELLIGENCE: GOAL-SETTING WORKSHEET 96
- REFLECTION QUESTIONS: REFLECTING ON YOUR GOALS 100
- FINAL THOUGHTS ON MOTIVATION AND GOAL SETTING 104

CHAPTER 7: EMPATHY: THE HEART OF EMOTIONAL INTELLIGENCE 105

- UNDERSTANDING EMPATHY 106
- THE IMPACT OF EMPATHY ON RELATIONSHIPS 110
  - Empathy in Professional Relationships 111
  - Empathy in Society 111
  - Empathy in Difficult Situations 112
- ENHANCING EMPATHETIC SKILLS 113
  - Understanding Others, Overcoming Biases, Nonverbal Communication, and Expressing Empathy 115
- OVERCOMING "EMPATHY" CHALLENGES 116
  - Boundaries and Empathy 117
- REFLECTION QUESTIONS 118
- EMPATHY CHALLENGES 121
  - Perspective Day 121
  - Listening Challenge 122
  - Compassionate Action 123
- RECOMMENDED BOOKS AND ARTICLES ON EMPATHY 123
  - Books 123
  - Articles 124

CHAPTER 8: READING SOCIAL CUES 125

- UNDERSTANDING SOCIAL CUES 126
- ACTIVE VS PASSIVE LISTENING 130
  - Distinguishing Between Active and Passive Listening 134
- READING THE ROOM: NAVIGATING SOCIAL SITUATIONS 135
- INTERACTIVE ELEMENT; LISTENING SKILLS EXERCISE 137
- REFLECTION AND SELF-ASSESSMENT: HOW WELL DO YOU READ NON-VERBAL CUES? 142
- FINAL THOUGHT ON THIS CHAPTER 144

CHAPTER 9: CULTURAL AND GENERATIONAL AWARENESS 145

- CONNECTING EMOTIONAL INTELLIGENCE, CULTURAL, AND GENERATIONAL AWARENESS ... 146
  - Cultural Awareness 149
  - Exercise: Building Emotional Intelligence in Cultural Awareness 152
  - Generational Awareness 153
  - Exercise: Building Emotional Intelligence in Generational Awareness 157
- FURTHER RESOURCES 159

- Books *159*
- Articles and Research Papers *159*
- REFLECTION QUESTIONS: EMOTIONAL INTELLIGENCE, CULTURAL, AND GENERATIONAL DIFFERENCES 160

CHAPTER 10: BUILDING STRONG RELATIONSHIPS 165

- HEALTHY RELATIONSHIPS UNDER THE MICROSCOPE 166
  - Trust and Honesty *166*
  - Mutual Respect *167*
  - Open Communication *168*
  - Empathy and Understanding *169*
  - Healthy Boundaries *170*
  - Effective Communication Strategies *171*
  - Conflict Resolution Strategies *175*
  - Interactive Element: Communication Skills Exercise *178*
- REFLECTION QUESTIONS 179

CHAPTER 11: EMOTIONAL INTELLIGENCE AT WORK 185

- LEADING WITH EMOTIONAL INTELLIGENCE 186
  - Examples of Emotional Intelligence in the Workplace *190*
  - How to Improve Emotional Intelligence in the Workplace *192*

CHAPTER 12: EMOTIONAL INTELLIGENCE IN FAMILY LIFE 195

- THE HEART OF THE FAMILY 196
- BUILDING EI IN FAMILY LIFE 199
- PARENTING WITH EMOTIONAL INTELLIGENCE 201
- NAVIGATING FAMILY CONFLICTS 203
- FAMILY DYNAMICS EXERCISE: EMOTIONAL CHECK-IN CIRCLE 206
- REFLECTION QUESTIONS: APPLYING EMOTIONAL INTELLIGENCE IN FAMILY RELATIONSHIPS 208

CHAPTER 13: OVERCOMING COMMON EMOTIONAl INTELLIGENCE CHALLENGES 213

- UNDERSTANDING EMOTIONAL INTELLIGENCE CHALLENGES 214
  - Lack of Self-Awareness *215*
  - Building Self-Awareness *215*
  - Improving Emotional Regulation *215*
  - Developing Empathy *216*
  - Social Skills Enhancement *216*
  - Motivation and Persistence *216*
  - Resources and Support *217*
  - Sustaining Progress *217*
- DAILY REFLECTION JOURNALING EXERCISE: OVERCOMING EMOTIONAL INTELLIGENCE CHALLENGES 217

  Reflection Questions: Overcoming Challenges 220

CHAPTER 14: PLANNING FOR ON-GOING GROWTH 227

  An Ongoing Journey 228
    Commitment to Personal Growth 228
    Building on Your Knowledge 229
    Real-Life Application 229
    Practicing Empathy 230
    Handling Difficult Emotions 230
    Encouraging Supportive Environments 230
    Lifelong Learning 231
    Celebrating Progress 231
  Step-by-Step Plan for Ongoing Growth 232
  Weekly Activity Planner: Increased Emotional Intelligence 234
    Monday: Self-Reflection 234
    Tuesday: Journaling 235
    Wednesday: Active Listening 235
    Thursday: Expressing Gratitude 236
    Friday: Mindfulness Practice 236
    Saturday: Social Interaction 236
    Sunday: Goal Setting 237
  Reflection Questions: Ongoing Growth 237

CONCLUSION 243

MY EMOTIONAL INTELLIGENCE NOTES 247

MY EMOTIONAL INTELLIGENCE NOTES 249

MY EMOTIONAL INTELLIGENCE NOTES 251

REFERENCES 253

Introduction

Some of the greatest moments in human history were fueled by emotional intelligence.
—Adam Grant

When it comes to learning and growing, age is just a number. No matter how many candles you have on your birthday cake, there is still plenty of room to develop new skills, gain fresh insights, and try new things.

Learning is all about opening yourself up to change and improvement, no matter where you are in life. It is like a little nudge, encouraging you to embrace new opportunities and challenges, showing that lifelong learning is possible and something to be excited about.

Emotional Intelligence (EI) is like having a superpower that is all about emotions, both yours and those of the people around you. It is not just about being in touch with your feelings. It is about really understanding what you are feeling, why you are feeling it, and how those emotions affect your thoughts and actions.

But it doesn't stop there. EI also means being able to tune into other people's emotions. It is like having an emotional radar that helps you pick up on how others are feeling, even if they are not saying it out loud. This greatly affects how you connect with people, build relationships, and navigate social situations.

So, why does this matter? Because life is full of emotions, yours and everyone else's. When you have a handle on your EI, you are better equipped to manage stress, communicate more effectively, and make choices that lead to better outcomes for everyone involved. It is not just about being intellectually smart but about being emotionally smart, which is often the key to living a happier, more balanced life.

EI matters because, let's face it, life is messy, and emotions are a big part of that mess. Whether you are dealing with stress at work or home, navigating tricky relationships, or trying to make it through a tough day, your emotions are always along for the ride. That is where EI comes in.

High EI is like having a personal guide to help you navigate life's emotional ups and downs. It helps you understand your feelings to better manage them instead of letting them control you. Imagine staying calm when things get heated or finding the right words in a difficult conversation. That is the power of EI.

But it is not just about you; EI also helps you connect with others. It is about picking up on what other people are feeling, even if they are not saying it outright, and responding in a thoughtful and kind way. This can make a huge difference in your relationships, whether it is with family, friends, or coworkers.

In short, EI matters since it helps you handle life with grace, make better decisions, build stronger relationships, and live with balance and well-being. It is a skill and a way of life that makes everything easier and more meaningful.

This book explores EI, breaks down its core components, and gives you practical strategies for developing your EI. From self-awareness to social skills, you will be given tools that are not just useful but immediately applicable.

Let's get started on a journey into the world of EI. Don't worry—this isn't some dry, academic slog. Think of it as a friendly chat, where you will pick up valuable insights along the way. You will learn what EI is, why it matters, and—most importantly—how to develop it in your own life.

Each chapter is packed with practical tips, relatable examples, and easy-to-follow strategies you can use immediately. Whether you want to improve your relationships, handle stress better, or understand yourself more, this book is here to help.

By the end, you won't just know what emotional intelligence is—you will live it. So, get comfortable, grab a cup of coffee, and explore how EI can be your secret weapon for a happier, more balanced life.

Chapter 1:

Emotional Intelligence 101

You need emotional intelligence to be happy, to take risks, to be competitive, and to look forward, not backwards. –Deborah Meaden

At 37, Claire faced an unexpected situation. She had a partner, great kids, a decent job, awesome friends, and a cozy home straight out of a Pinterest board. Yet, despite it all, something felt amiss—not in a dramatic way, but as a quiet, nagging feeling she couldn't shake.

On a Wednesday afternoon, during a meeting, Claire's boss made a comment that irritated her. Usually, she would ignore it or smile politely while feeling angry inside. This time was different; she realized she didn't even know why it upset her. That night, while scrolling through Instagram, she came across a post about emotional intelligence. The post encouraged people to go out and buy a book by the name of *Emotional Intelligence: Your Ultimate Hands-On Guide*.

"Emotional what?" she muttered to herself, intrigued. Many people who responded to the post talked about how the book helped them become more in tune with their emotions and understand how they drive their thoughts, actions, and reactions. Claire started reading the comments and found herself nodding to strangers' stories about how reading this book helped them feel more grounded and in control.

"Maybe this is what I am missing," she thought. Just like that, Claire followed the link and purchased the book online.

One sunny morning, her doorbell rang, and she answered the door. This was the delivery of her book. Excitedly, she unwrapped her parcel; her journey into emotional intelligence had officially begun. Claire realized she was about to figure out who she wanted to be.

Origins of Emotional Intelligence

Emotional intelligence has been around for a long time, but it became popular in the 1990s thanks to psychologists Peter Salovey, John Mayer, and Daniel Goleman's 1995 book *Emotional Intelligence*. Since then, research has shown the positive impact that EI can have on everything from personal relationships to professional success (*Emotional Intelligence*, 2019).

EI is the ability to understand and manage your own emotions while recognizing and influencing the emotions of others. First introduced by researchers John Mayer and Peter Salovey, EI became widely known through Daniel Goleman's work.

Goleman highlighted that the most effective leaders share high EI, noting that while IQ and technical skills matter, EI is key to leadership success. Research shows that employees with strong EI handle stress better, resolve conflicts, and show empathy, making it a crucial factor in job performance and workplace success (Golis, 2017).

EI is all about recognizing, understanding, and managing emotions in a way that helps you navigate all areas of your life well. It is not just about knowing your feelings but understanding why you feel that way. EI uses that insight so you can make better decisions and handle everyday situations better.

Understanding the basics of EI provides a solid foundation for exploring how to develop and apply these skills in various areas of your life. The components of EI typically include:

- self-awareness
- self-regulation
- empathy
- social skills
- motivation

Let's have a look at each of these.

Self-Awareness

Self-awareness is about recognizing and understanding your emotions and how they impact your thoughts and behavior. It is about being in tune with your feelings and why and how those feelings affect your actions and interactions. For instance, if you are anxious about a big presentation, self-awareness allows you to pinpoint that anxiety and understand how it might influence your performance or communication.

By understanding your emotions, you can identify patterns in your behavior and reactions. This insight helps you manage your responses more effectively, leading to better interactions with others and a more balanced emotional state. For example, knowing you are prone to feeling defensive during feedback can help you approach criticism more openly.

Self-awareness is foundational to personal growth and effective communication. You can develop greater awareness through:

- **Journaling:** Regularly writing about your daily experiences and emotional reactions helps track patterns and triggers. Reflect on your feelings and how they influence your behavior.

- **Mindfulness:** Practice mindfulness techniques like meditation or deep breathing. These help you become more aware of your emotions in the present moment and reduce impulsive reactions.

- **Feedback seeking:** Ask for feedback from trusted friends, family, or colleagues about how your emotions affect your behavior. This external perspective can enhance your self-awareness.

Self-Regulation

Self-regulation involves managing your emotions in a healthy, controlled way. It means staying calm and composed, even in stressful situations, and controlling impulsive reactions. For example, if you are feeling frustrated during a team meeting, self-regulation helps you respond calmly and thoughtfully rather than reacting with anger.

Effective self-regulation is important for stress management and decision-making. It helps prevent emotional outbursts and hasty decisions that could harm relationships or professional outcomes. By regulating your emotions, you can maintain a clearer, more rational perspective, which supports better problem-solving and conflict resolution.

You can develop self-regulation through:

- **Deep breathing:** Practice breathing exercises to calm your nervous system and gain control during stressful moments.

- **Cognitive restructuring:** Challenge and reframe negative thoughts that contribute to emotional reactions. For example, if you are anxious about a deadline, focus on the steps to meet it rather than stressing about potential failure.

- **Pause and reflect:** Before responding in emotionally charged situations, take a moment to pause and consider your response. This brief reflection can help you choose a more measured and effective reaction.

Empathy

When you are empathetic, you can understand and share others' feelings. It involves putting yourself in someone else's shoes and grasping their emotional experience from their perspective. For instance, if a friend is going through a tough time, empathy allows you to connect with their feelings and offer appropriate support.

Empathy enhances relationships and teamwork by fostering trust and mutual understanding. It helps you respond to others' needs and emotions more effectively, strengthening connections and collaborative environments. Empathetic people are often better at resolving conflicts, building rapport, and improving personal and professional relationships.

You can develop greater empathy through:

- **Active listening:** Focus on truly listening to others without interrupting. Show that you are engaged, maintain eye contact, and reflect on what you have heard.

- **Perspective-taking:** Try to view situations from others' viewpoints. Ask yourself how you would feel if you were in their position and how you might want to be treated.

- **Empathy exercises:** Practice empathy by volunteering or taking part in activities that expose you to different perspectives and life experiences.

Social Skills

To survive in the world, one needs to have social skills; as they say, no man is an island. Strong social skills are important for building and maintaining personal and professional relationships. Having healthy social skills enables you to

- communicate well

- navigate social situations well.

- positively influence others

- lead well

- collaborate well

- handle disagreements
- resolve conflicts
- build healthy relationships

You can develop your social skills through:

- **Assertiveness training:** Learning to express your needs and opinions confidently and respectfully without being aggressive or passive.

- **Seeking feedback:** Asking for feedback on your social interactions to identify areas for improvement. It is important to be open to suggestions and use them to enhance your communication skills.

- **Practicing communication:** Engaging in social activities and working on how you interact with others. Join clubs, attend networking events, or participate in group discussions to build confidence and proficiency.

Motivation

Motivation uses emotional energy to pursue your goals and maintain a positive attitude. It involves having personal goals, staying focused, and overcoming obstacles with enthusiasm and perseverance. Motivation can be broadly classified into two main types. These two categories can help explain why you take action and what drives behavior: intrinsic and extrinsic motivation (SpriggHR, 2020).

Motivation type and definition	Example	Characteristics
• Intrinsic motivation comes from within. It's driven by personal satisfaction or the inherent enjoyment of the activity itself.	• Learning a new language is good because you enjoy the challenge, or playing a sport is good because it's fun, not because you're trying to win a prize.	• The activity is rewarding in itself. • Focuses on personal growth, curiosity, or inner desires. • Linked to feelings of competence and autonomy.
• Extrinsic motivation is driven by external rewards or to avoid negative outcomes. It comes from outside the individual.	• Working a job to earn money or studying to get good grades.	• The activity is done to achieve an external reward or to avoid a punishment. • Often linked to material rewards, recognition, or approval from others.

Boosting your motivation can be a challenge and takes work, but there are several ways in which you can do so. Let's look at a few ways:

- **Set clear, achievable goals:** Yes, large goals can feel overwhelming, so break them down into smaller, manageable steps and focus on completing one at a time. Be sure to monitor your progress. Seeing how far you have come will inspire you to keep going.

- **Find your "why":** You must understand exactly why a task or goal is important. Remember to have a strong reason behind your actions, as this can fuel your drive. Focus on intrinsic (internal) motivators—like personal satisfaction or passion. External rewards can help, but they might not sustain motivation long-term.

- **Routine matters:** Develop habits and routines that incorporate your tasks. Once a behavior becomes automatic, motivation is less needed to initiate it. Also, specific time slots for particular tasks should be dedicated to reduce procrastination.

- **Reward yourself:** Reward yourself for completing tasks, no matter how small; doing this will reinforce positive behavior and keep your motivation levels up. Remember to incorporate breaks or enjoyable activities as a reward after productive sessions.

- **Visualizing success:** Picture yourself achieving your goals and the positive outcomes of this achievement. Visualization can boost motivation and make the path to success feel more attainable.

- **Positive affirmations:** Use positive affirmations to reinforce your confidence and maintain a hopeful outlook. Remind yourself of your strengths and past successes.

- **Get rid of distractions**: Limit distractions to help you stay focused. This could mean turning off notifications or creating a dedicated workplace.

- **Surround yourself with positivity:** Spend time with people who encourage you. Their energy can uplift your own and help keep you motivated. Practice being kind to yourself, especially when things do not go as planned.

- **Take care of your health:** Believe it or not, physical activity can boost your energy levels and improve your mood, directly impacting motivation. A healthy diet and good sleep are critical for maintaining energy and focus.

When you are highly motivated, you stay committed to your objectives, even when faced with setbacks or challenges. It fuels your passion and determination, making overcoming obstacles and reaching your goals easier.

Debunking Common Myths

By debunking common myths about EI, you will see that it is a multifaceted skill set that can be developed and applied in all areas of your life. Whether you are aiming to improve your relationships or advance in your career, enhancing your EI is a powerful step toward achieving your goals.

Myth 1: EI Is the Same as IQ

One of the most common misconceptions is that EI and intelligence quotient (IQ) are interchangeable. In reality, they are distinct yet complementary forms of intelligence. IQ measures cognitive abilities like logical reasoning, problem-solving, and analytical thinking, whereas

EI is about understanding and managing emotions, both your own and others.

Developing both EI and IQ is important for overall success. While IQ might get you through a job's technical aspects, EI helps you connect with others, manage stress, and lead effectively. In today's world, where collaboration and communication are key, balancing IQ and EI can make you more personally and professionally effective.

Myth 2: You Are Either Born With EI, or You Are Not

Another widespread myth is that EI is an innate trait you either have or don't. The truth is, EI is a skill that can be cultivated and enhanced over time, much like learning to play an instrument or mastering a new language. With practice, anyone can improve their EI, regardless of their starting point.

This reality is empowering because it means you have control over your emotional growth. Whether you feel naturally empathetic or not, you can engage in activities that develop your EI, like mindfulness, active listening, and self-reflection. The growth potential is unlimited, so there is no reason to feel discouraged if you think your EI could improve. There is always room to grow.

Myth 3: EI Is All About Being Nice and Empathetic

While empathy is an important aspect of EI, it goes far beyond just being nice or understanding others' feelings. It also includes self-awareness, self-regulation, motivation, and social skills. A person with high EI is empathetic and effective in various social settings.

Recognizing the full scope of EI can help you develop a more balanced approach to EI. For example, self-regulation allows you to stay composed under pressure, while social skills enable you to navigate complex interpersonal dynamics. Understanding that EI is more than just being kind opens new avenues for personal and professional growth.

Myth 4: High EI Means You Never Experience Negative Emotions

A high EI doesn't mean you are immune to negative emotions like anger, sadness, or frustration. Instead, it means you are better equipped to manage these emotions healthily and constructively. People with high EI still experience the full range of emotions, but they can recognize these feelings, understand their triggers, and choose how to respond rather than react impulsively.

This myth often leads people to believe that EI is about suppressing negative emotions, which is not the case. The key is to acknowledge and manage these emotions effectively. For example, if you are feeling angry, a high EI helps you express that anger in a way that is assertive but not destructive, leading to better outcomes in both personal and professional situations.

Myth 5: EI Is Only Useful in Personal Relationships

While EI is valuable in personal relationships, its importance extends far beyond that. In professional settings, EI is important for effective leadership, teamwork, and conflict resolution. Leaders with high EI can inspire and motivate their teams, foster a positive work environment, and handle crises calmly and clearly.

Understanding the role of EI in the workplace can significantly enhance your career prospects. Whether leading a team, collaborating with colleagues, or navigating office politics, applying EI skills can help you achieve better outcomes and build stronger professional relationships. By developing your EI, you are improving your personal life and setting yourself up for success in your career (Tunnell, 2024).

Quick Self-Assessment Quiz

This self-assessment quiz will help you understand your EI skills. It is a quick, easy way to identify your strengths and areas that need more attention. Remember, this isn't about judgment; it is about growth. By understanding where you stand today, you can enhance your EI and become more emotionally aware, resilient, and effective in your interactions.

Quiz Instructions

This quiz consists of ten statements related to different aspects of EI. For each statement, rate yourself on a scale from 1 to 5, where:

- **1 = Strongly Disagree**
- **2 =Disagree**
- **3 = Neutral**
- **4 = Agree**
- **5 = Strongly Agree**

Quiz Questions

1. I can easily recognize my own emotions and understand why I feel a certain way.

2. I stay calm and collected even when stressed or facing a difficult situation.

3. I am good at picking up on other people's emotions, even if they don't say anything.

4. I can handle conflicts and disagreements in a way that respects both my feelings and those of others.

5. I often empathize with others and offer support when they need it.

6. I can communicate my feelings and needs clearly and effectively without creating unnecessary tension.

7. I know how my emotions affect my decisions and actions, and I strive to make thoughtful choices.

8. I am open to feedback about my emotional responses and am willing to make changes if needed.

9. I can adapt to changing circumstances without becoming overly upset or stressed.

10. I regularly reflect on my emotions and behavior to improve my interactions with others.

Scoring:

Once you have completed the quiz, add your score to get a total. The possible score range is 10 to 50.

- **40-50:** You have a strong foundation in EI. Your self-awareness, empathy, and ability to manage emotions are well-developed, but there is always room for further growth and refinement.

- **30-39:** You have a good grasp of EI, but there are some areas where you could benefit from more focus and development. Consider which statements you scored lower on, and explore ways to enhance those skills.

- **20-29:** Your EI is developing, but significant room exists for improvement. Identifying your strengths and working actively on weaker areas will help you become more emotionally adept.

- **10-19:** It is clear that EI is an area you could greatly benefit from focusing on. Don't be discouraged; this is an opportunity for meaningful personal growth. Explore the basics of EI and work on building these essential skills.

Now, based on your score, reflect on which aspects of EI you would like to improve. Whether you want to become more self-aware, improve your relationships, or handle stress more effectively, this quiz begins your journey toward greater EI.

Reflection Questions: Understanding Emotional Intelligence

What is your current understanding of EI? How do you perceive its role in your personal and professional life?

Reflect on the strategies you use to handle your emotions. Are they working well for you? Do you find yourself in control of your reactions, or are there situations where you struggle?

How do you recognize and respond to others' emotions? Consider your interactions with others. How attuned are you to their emotions? Do you find it easy to empathize and respond appropriately, or is this an area where you could improve?

How can improving your emotional intelligence benefit you? Could it help you navigate stressful situations, improve relationships, or boost your career prospects?

Emotional intelligence has various components: self-awareness, self-regulation, empathy, social skills, and motivation. What aspects of emotional intelligence would you like to improve?

Chapter 2:

The Science Behind Emotions

> *Emotional intelligence is your ability to recognize and understand emotions in yourself and others and your ability to use this awareness to manage your behavior and relationships.* –Travis Bradberry

Claire read the Introduction and Chapter 1 of **Emotional Intelligence: Your Ultimate Hands-On Guide** the first evening. The more Claire read, the more curious she was. The old Claire used to dismiss or suppress her feelings with an extra latte, but this new Claire was learning to tune in and pay attention. That curiosity led her down a rabbit hole she never saw coming: the science behind emotions.

One afternoon, sitting with a cup of tea and a notebook, Claire learned that emotions were not just random moods that popped up to make her life more complicated. They had a real biological reason for being there. She discovered that emotions are triggered in the brain, mainly the amygdala, where they help you respond to threats and opportunities.

"So, my brain is trying to help me, not just stress me out?" she thought, amazed. What a revelation! Claire continued reading and learned that emotions also send signals to the rest of the body. For example, her heart rate increased when she was anxious, and she felt a burst of energy when she was excited. These emotions were helpful messengers, not problems to fix. However, she had spent most of her life ignoring them, or worse, letting them run the show without understanding their role.

"Okay, brain. I see you," Claire muttered, half-smiling. "If I start paying attention to these messengers instead of fighting them, I can figure out why I get defensive in meetings, feel drained after certain conversations, or why small things trigger big emotions."

The more that she read, the more Claire started to see that emotional intelligence was not just about being better at handling feelings. It was about decoding her brain's language, understanding what her body was telling her, and using that information to live a more balanced and intentional life. She jotted down a quick note to herself, "Emotions are not my enemies, they are data."

More Than Feelings

Emotions are far more than just feelings; they are a fundamental aspect of human experience and are integral to your well-being. They profoundly influence your actions and thoughts, from the satisfaction of achieving a goal to the disappointment of facing a setback. They enable you to forge connections with others, tackle challenges, and navigate life's complexities. While, at times, emotions may seem overwhelming, they are deeply rooted in the brain's biology and are essential for your overall well-being.

It's no secret that emotions can significantly impact your behavior. They have the power to influence the way you see the world, the choices you make, and how you engage with others. For example, feeling joyful can lead to a more optimistic outlook, while experiencing frustration may cloud your judgment. Emotions not only color your perceptions but also influence the decisions you make in various situations.

They play a powerful role in decision-making, often guiding choices and judgments. Though people may believe they make decisions based on logic, research shows that emotions are deeply intertwined with the process (Ratson, 2023). Emotions serve as shortcuts, helping people to assess situations and make judgments without extensive deliberation. For example, fear might lead to avoiding risky situations, while excitement could push someone to pursue new opportunities.

The interplay between logic and emotion in decision-making is complex. Logic evaluates options based on facts, while emotions add personal relevance and urgency. Emotions can tip the scales when logic alone cannot provide a clear answer. They can enhance decision-making by providing insights into what matters, signaling needs, desires, and priorities. However, intense or misinformed emotions can cloud judgment and lead to regrettable, impulsive decisions. Balancing logic and emotion is crucial for making well-rounded decisions that serve immediate and long-term goals.

Understanding the science behind your emotions can give you insight into how they are triggered and manifest and why they play a vital role in your life. This knowledge can empower you to navigate your emotional experiences better, handle challenges, and foster healthier relationships.

The Brain's Role in Emotions

The human brain is the most complex organ in the body. It controls your emotions and every other vital function and chemical reaction needed for survival. With over a billion neurons and countless connections, the brain orchestrates everything.

A key player in your emotional and memory processing is the limbic system, which includes several important parts:

- **Hypothalamus**: Located near the pituitary gland, it plays a crucial role in releasing hormones and regulating body temperature, among other functions.

- **Thalamus**: Acts as a relay station for sensory information (except smell), processing and directing it to the appropriate areas of the brain.

- **Hippocampus**: Essential for learning, memory, and emotional responses.

- **Pituitary gland**: Produces various hormones and controls other hormone glands, like the thyroid, adrenal glands, ovaries, and testicles.

- **Amygdala**: The area of the brain where emotions are processed and given meaning (Seladi-Schulman, 2018).

Chemistry of Emotions

You have likely noticed how your mood can shape the entire course of your day. Whether you wake up feeling cheerful and optimistic or down and irritable, your mood has a powerful influence on how you think, feel, and experience the world around you.

Ordinary tasks can seem enjoyable, and challenges may feel more manageable when you are in a positive mood. On the other hand, when you are feeling low, those same tasks can feel overwhelming, and even small inconveniences can seem like major obstacles.

But what exactly is happening inside your brain when your mood shifts? These mood changes are not just random; they are driven by complex chemical and neurological processes in the brain. Various factors, including hormone levels, neurotransmitter activity, and external stimuli, all play a role in determining how you feel at any given moment. Understanding these processes can help you better manage your mood and improve your well-being.

Chemical reactions in your brain influence your emotions. Neurotransmitters like oxytocin, serotonin, dopamine, and endorphins constantly affect your emotions. Understanding their interactions can help you manage your emotional health through lifestyle changes, therapy, or other interventions, benefiting your mental well-being.

Key chemicals regulating positive emotions include:
- **Serotonin:** Also known as the "feel-good neurotransmitter," is crucial for happiness and mood stability. It is produced from tryptophan, which regulates sleep and appetite and is found throughout the body. Balanced serotonin levels are essential for overall health. You can naturally boost serotonin through diet, sunlight, supplements, exercise, and stress management.

Imbalanced levels can lead to health issues, so maintaining healthy levels is important.

- **Dopamine:** This neurotransmitter is produced by the hypothalamus and is important for experiencing pleasure. It reinforces positive behaviors and emotions, driving you to seek rewarding experiences. Boosting dopamine levels naturally can be done through activities like meditation, listening to music, eating protein-rich foods, exercising, spending time in the sun, and getting enough sleep. These practices help maintain healthy dopamine levels, supporting overall well-being and motivation.

- **Endorphins:** These opioid peptides, produced by the hypothalamus and pituitary glands, act as natural painkillers in the brain. They are released in response to pain or stress, blocking nerve cells from receiving pain signals and allowing the body to function in challenging situations. Exercise, like powerwalking, running, or hiking, boosts endorphin levels. Other ways to stimulate endorphin release include eating dark chocolate, acupuncture, meditation, listening to music, and practicing mindfulness, all enhancing mood and overall well-being.

- **Oxytocin:** Also known as the "love hormone," is produced in the hypothalamus and released by the pituitary gland. It helps in childbirth, labor, and lactation and is linked to maternal bonding. Additionally, oxytocin acts as a chemical messenger in the brain, influencing behaviors like trust and recognition. Its release triggers more oxytocin production (Akene, 2020).

Understanding how emotions influence decisions can help you make choices that align with your values and long-term goals, avoiding regrets. Consider how emotions influence decisions like buying a car. While someone might logically weigh fuel efficiency and cost, their emotional attachment to a brand or the excitement of a sporty model might lead them to a less practical choice. This can result in satisfaction or buyer's remorse if the car doesn't meet their needs.

In relationships, emotions often guide decisions. Someone might stay in an unhealthy relationship due to love or fear of loneliness despite logical reasons to leave. Conversely, positive emotions like joy and respect can lead to long-term happiness.

Even in the workplace, emotions affect decisions. A promotion may seem logical for better pay, but if it increases stress or cuts into family time, emotions might lead someone to decline for the sake of work-life balance.

The Difference Between IQ and EI

Understanding the difference between IQ and EI is key to recognizing how each contributes to success, whether in academics, the workplace, or personal relationships.

IQ (intellectual abilities and cognitive skills)	**EI (ability to recognize, understand, and manage emotions)**
• logical problem-solving	• identify emotions
• planning and strategizing	• empathize
• understanding abstract concepts	• adapt behavior
• learning and adapting	• control impulses
• language skills	• resolve conflicts
	• communicate effectively

How Are IQ and EI Measured?

Higher IQ scores have historically been associated with better academic performance, higher salaries, and improved job outcomes. However, recent studies have questioned the extent of these links, suggesting that IQ alone may not be a complete predictor of success.

On the other hand, EI has been linked to job success, more fulfilling relationships, and better stress management. Research, including a 2019 review, indicates that EI can enhance your ability to recover from acute stress more effectively (Houston, 2019).

Both IQ and EI significantly impact your quality of life and achievements. Developing and understanding both types of intelligence can be beneficial for achieving success across various aspects of life. Balancing and enhancing both IQ and EI may provide a more comprehensive approach to personal and professional growth.

While IQ measures cognitive abilities, EI focuses on emotional and social skills, both crucial for success in different areas of life. The accuracy of IQ and EI measurements is a topic of considerable debate, with various factors potentially influencing test outcomes. Environmental conditions can all impact test results, for example:

- economic status
- social inequalities
- access to education
- childhood nutrition
- childhood trauma

IQ tests typically assess two types of intelligence:
- **Crystallized intelligence**: Based on acquired knowledge and verbal abilities, often improving with age.

- **Fluid intelligence**: Involves reasoning, abstract thinking, and problem-solving without relying on pre-existing knowledge.

Other IQ tests, like the Universal Nonverbal Intelligence Test and Raven's Progressive Matrices, aim to measure intelligence independently of verbal skills.

Common IQ measurement tests include:

- Stanford-Binet Intelligence Scale (Stanford-Binet Test, 2019)
- Woodcock-Johnson III Tests of Cognitive Abilities (Cherry, MSEd, 2018)
- Wechsler Adult Intelligence Scale (Cherry, 2022)

EI tests often evaluate:

- **Ability intelligence**: how effectively you use social and emotional skills to solve problems.
- **Trait intelligence**: Your self-assessed typical behaviors and responses.

Many EI assessments measure competencies in five areas:

- self-awareness
- self-regulation
- motivation
- empathy
- social skills (Cherry, 2023)

Common EI tests include:

- Mayer-Salovey-Caruso Emotional Intelligence Tests

- Situational Tests of Emotional Management

- Situational Tests of Emotional Understanding

- Diagnostic Analysis of Nonverbal Accuracy (*Emotional Intelligence Test*, n.d.)

Can You Improve Your IQ and EI?

The debate continues about whether IQ can be improved significantly. Some scientists argue that IQ can be enhanced through certain interventions, while others suggest that measuring a real increase in basic intelligence is challenging. However, strategies do exist to potentially boost both IQ and EI.

Strategies to enhance IQ:

- **Build problem-solving skills:**

    o **Training programs:** Evidence supports the idea that creative problem-solving and creativity training programs can improve cognitive skills (Ritter et al., 2020).

    o **Self-study:** Books like Michael Michalko's *Thinkertoys* offer techniques to enhance creative thinking.

- **Practice relational framing:**

    o **Activities:** Engaging in activities that involve comparing and contrasting ideas, sequencing events, analyzing opposites, and finding relationships between unrelated images can improve general intelligence. A 2016 study found that students who practiced these activities significantly improved IQ tests (Lynch, 2022).

Strategies to enhance EI:

- **Workplace EI training:**

    - **Training programs:** EI-related training can improve teamwork, conflict management, job performance, and job satisfaction. Participating in such programs can enhance various aspects of EI.

- **Reading:**

    - **Empathy development:** Reading about diverse experiences, whether through fiction or non-fiction, can improve social thinking and empathy, crucial components of EI.

Incorporating these strategies into your routine may help boost your IQ and EI, leading to overall personal and professional growth.

Practical Applications of Emotional Science

Understanding the science behind emotions can significantly enhance various aspects of daily life, from personal relationships to professional success. By recognizing how emotions influence our thoughts and behaviors, we can better navigate our emotional experiences and make more informed decisions.

One of the primary benefits of understanding emotional science is improved emotional awareness. By being aware of our emotions as they arise, we can identify triggers and patterns, allowing us to respond more thoughtfully rather than impulsively. For example, if we recognize that stress often leads to irritability, we can take proactive steps to manage stress before it impacts our interactions with others.

To enhance emotional awareness and regulation, consider the following tips:

- **Practice mindfulness**: Mindfulness techniques, like meditation or deep breathing, help increase awareness of your emotional state and create a space between your emotions and reactions. This can lead to more measured responses in challenging situations.

- **Reflect regularly**: Reflecting on your emotional experiences through journaling can help you better understand your emotions and how they influence your decisions. Regular reflection also promotes self-awareness and emotional growth.

- **Develop coping strategies**: Identifying effective ways to manage strong emotions, including exercise, talking to a friend, or engaging in a creative activity, can help you regulate your emotions and prevent them from overwhelming you.

Integrating emotional science into decision-making processes has numerous benefits. By acknowledging the role of emotions in our choices, we can make decisions that align more closely with our values and long-term goals. This balanced approach, which considers logical reasoning and emotional insight, often leads to more satisfying and effective outcomes.

Bringing emotional awareness into your daily life will enhance your personal well-being and improve interpersonal relationships, work performance, and overall life satisfaction. Understanding and applying the science of emotions equip us with the tools to lead a more balanced and fulfilling life.

Reflection Questions

Think about a recent decision you made. How did your emotions influence it? Did your feelings lead you to choose a particular option, or did they cloud your judgment?

Can you recall when your EI helped you in a challenging situation? Perhaps you successfully navigated a difficult conversation, resolved a conflict, or supported someone. How did your emotional awareness and skills contribute to a positive outcome?

Consider your usual methods for handling intense emotions, whether they involve mindfulness practices, talking to someone you trust, or engaging in physical activity. Evaluate which strategies are most effective for you and how they help you maintain emotional balance. Are there any new techniques you could use to improve your emotional regulation?

Chapter 3:

Self-Awareness: Know Thyself

Self-awareness is a trait - or maybe 'practice' is the more accurate way to put it - that everyone can always improve at. It is part emotional intelligence, part perceptiveness, part critical thinking. It means knowing your weaknesses, of course, but it also means knowing your strengths and what motivates you. –Neil Blumenthal

As Claire continued her unique journey with emotional intelligence, she noticed subtle changes in her life. Yes, there were still challenging moments where she felt overwhelmed or annoyed, but instead of reacting on autopilot, she paused. That pause, she realized, was the first real sign that something inside her was shifting.

After a particularly challenging day at work, Claire took a walk to clear her mind. Her emotions were running high: frustration, stress, and maybe even a touch of resentment, but instead of letting them simmer, she tried something new. She asked herself, "What am I feeling right now? And, more importantly, why?

When Claire got home, she took a hot shower and sat down to continue reading her book. Today, Claire learned that self-awareness was like the foundation of emotional intelligence. It meant recognizing and understanding your emotions as they happened instead of reacting to them. Curious, Claire started practicing this idea. Whenever she felt a strong emotion, she would pause and check in with herself, trying to name the feeling and trace where it was coming from.

It was a strange process at first. It was like holding up a mirror to her inner world, but the more that Claire did it, the more clarity she gained. For example, when her boss interrupted her during a meeting, she felt her usual annoyance flare up. But this time, instead of stewing in it all day, she asked herself, "Why does this bother me so much?" After reflecting, she realized it wasn't about her boss being rude; it was about her insecurity that perhaps she wasn't being taken seriously enough.

This realization hit her hard, but it was also empowering. Instead of blaming others for her emotional reactions, Claire took ownership of them. She became more aware of her emotional patterns, such as getting defensive when feeling undervalued or avoiding tough conversations due to her fear of conflict.

Claire's newfound self-awareness brought immediate benefits. She felt more in control, grounded, and able to observe and understand her emotions. Her relationships improved, as she stopped snapping at her partner over small things by recognizing her stress and communicating instead of lashing out.

Claire started to notice a difference at work. During a team meeting, she listened instead of reacting when someone gave her feedback that would have normally triggered defensiveness. She acknowledged the feedback for what it was: an opportunity to improve and not a personal attack. And just like that, work no longer felt so stressful.

Suddenly, Claire realized that self-awareness was like having a secret superpower. It allowed her to step back from her emotions and see things clearly. Additionally, it allowed her to make choices that aligned with who she wanted to be, not just how she felt in the moment.

Mirror Within

Taking a journey of developing self-awareness is where you will truly discover and understand the most important person in your life: yourself. Self-awareness is more than knowing what foods or hobbies you like; it is about digging deeper into your emotions. Understanding why you react the way you do and identifying the triggers that set off certain feelings. You can think of self-awareness as a powerful tool that helps you navigate life with greater ease, clarity, and confidence.

Self-awareness is all about understanding yourself on a deeper level: your emotions, thoughts, and behaviors. It is like holding up a mirror to your inner self, allowing you to see what is really going on beneath the surface. When you are self-aware, you can recognize what drives your reactions and how your emotions influence your decisions.

It is also the foundation of personal growth. The more you know about yourself, the better equipped you are to manage your emotions, handle stress, and make decisions that align with your true values. Enhancing your self-awareness isn't just about feeling more in control; it is about improving your overall well-being. By getting to know yourself better, you will find that navigating life's ups and downs becomes a lot easier.

Developing self-awareness or working on any form of personal growth requires self-reflection. What is self-reflection? Self-reflection is taking the time to pause and think about your thoughts, emotions, and actions. It is about looking inward and asking yourself, "Why did I react that way?" or "What do I really want in this situation?"

You can think of self-reflection as an important gateway to self-awareness. When you take the time to check in with your emotions regularly, you start to understand the underlying reasons behind your feelings and behavior, which is key to personal growth.

Self-Reflection Matters

Self-reflection is important because it allows you to step back and examine your thoughts, feelings, and actions with a clear mind. This will help you understand your behaviors, recognize patterns, and gain insights into what drives you. Let's look at why taking time for self-reflection is so important for enhancing self-awareness and leading a more intentional life.

- **Understanding your core values, beliefs, and goals**: When you reflect, you understand what truly matters. This helps you make decisions that align with your values and move toward your goals with purpose.

- **Gaining insight into past behaviors**: Reflecting on past experiences allows you to see patterns in your behavior, both positive and negative. This insight is invaluable for making changes that lead to better outcomes in the future.

- **Improving emotional intelligence**: Self-reflection sharpens your EI by helping you understand your emotions and how they affect your interactions. This, in turn, improves your relationships and decision-making.

Practical Tips for Effective Self-Reflection

By regularly practicing self-reflection, you will deepen your understanding of yourself and lay a solid foundation for personal development. Effective self-reflection can be a game-changer for personal growth, but it is important to approach it in a way that is both practical and impactful.

Let's explore some simple yet powerful tips to help you make the most of your self-reflection practice. From setting aside regular time to using prompts that guide your thoughts, these tips will ensure your reflections are insightful and actionable.

- **Make time for it**: Set aside regular time for self-reflection, whether it is a few minutes each day or a longer session each week. Consistency is key to developing this habit.

- **Use prompts or questions**: Sometimes, knowing where to start is hard. Use prompts like, "What was the highlight of my day?" or "What could I have handled better?" to guide your reflections.

- **Reflect on both successes and challenges**: Don't just focus on what went wrong. Celebrate your successes, no matter how small, and reflect on what contributed to those wins. This balanced approach helps you grow more effectively.

Identifying Emotional Triggers

Emotional triggers are those specific situations, words, or behaviors that provoke a strong emotional response from you, often out of proportion to the actual event. Think of triggers as buttons that, when you press them, can instantly set off an intense reaction, whether it is anger, sadness, anxiety, or frustration. These reactions can impact your behavior and decision-making, often in ways that aren't helpful. Recognizing and understanding your triggers is key to managing your emotions better (Raypole, 2020).

Identifying emotional triggers is about understanding what causes your strong emotional reactions. These triggers can be specific events, comments, or situations that stir up intense feelings. Here are a few examples of things that commonly trigger strong emotional responses:

- **Criticism**: Whether it is constructive or not, criticism can feel like a personal attack, making you defensive or upset.

- **Failure**: Not meeting expectations, whether on your own or others, can trigger feelings of shame, disappointment, or frustration.

- **Stress**: High-pressure situations, tight deadlines, or overwhelming responsibilities can make you more reactive and emotionally sensitive.

- **Rejection**: Feeling rejected, whether in relationships, work, or social settings, can trigger feelings of inadequacy or hurt.

- **Conflict**: Disagreements or confrontations can quickly escalate if they hit a personal trigger, leading to heightened emotions and tension.

To manage your emotional triggers, you first need to identify them. But how do you pinpoint your personal triggers and use this knowledge to improve your emotional well-being? Here is how you can start:

- **Reflect on past reactions**: Think back to situations where you have had a strong emotional response. What was happening? Who was involved? These reflections can help you identify your triggers.

- **Journal your experiences**: Keep a journal where you note down moments when you felt triggered. Over time, you will see patterns that set you off.

- **Tune Into your body**: Your body often gives clues when triggered. Pay attention to physical signs like a racing heart, clenched fists, or a knot in your stomach. These can be indicators that something has triggered you emotionally.

Managing Emotional Triggers

Managing emotional triggers involves recognizing what sets off your strong reactions and learning how to respond calmly. By understanding your triggers, you can develop strategies to handle them effectively, reducing their impact on your emotions and behavior. This process helps you maintain better control over your responses and fosters a more balanced and thoughtful approach to challenging situations.

Let's explore practical techniques to manage your triggers and keep your emotional reactions in check. Here are some strategies to help you manage them so they don't control your reactions:

- **Practice mindfulness**: Mindfulness helps you become more aware of your triggers as they arise. By staying present, you can catch the trigger early before it triggers an automatic reaction.

- **Develop coping strategies**: When you recognize a trigger, have a few strategies to calm yourself. This could be as simple as taking deep breaths, stepping away from the situation, or counting to ten before responding.

- **Reframe negative thoughts**: Triggers are often linked to negative thoughts or beliefs. Challenge these thoughts by asking yourself, "Is this really true?" or "Am I overreacting?" Reframing your perspective can help you respond more calmly.

By understanding and managing your emotional triggers, you will gain more control over your reactions and improve your emotional well-being. This self-awareness will help you navigate difficult situations with greater ease and resilience.

Tools for Building Self-Awareness

Using tools to build self-awareness can be incredibly empowering. By incorporating practices like journaling, mindfulness, and seeking feedback, you can uncover deeper insights about yourself and how you interact with the world. This self-knowledge not only improves your emotional management but also enhances your decision-making and relationships.

Let's have a look at some practical tools that can help support you on your journey toward greater self-awareness and overall well-being.

Journaling

Journaling is a powerful tool for building self-awareness because it helps you get your thoughts and feelings out of your head and onto paper. By writing about your daily experiences, emotions, and reflections, you can clarify what's happening inside you. This practice helps you process your feelings and reveals patterns and insights that might not be obvious now.

Types of Journals

- **Daily reflections**: Write about your daily experiences, thoughts, and feelings. This helps you track how you feel daily and spot trends over time.

- **Gratitude journals**: Focus on what you are grateful for. This can shift your perspective to a more positive outlook and help you appreciate the good in your life.

- **Emotional tracking**: Note down your emotional states and triggers. This can help you identify what's causing certain feelings and how to address them.

Tips for Effective Journaling

- **Be consistent**: Set aside a regular time each day or week to journal. Consistency helps you build a habit and get the most out of your reflections.

- **Be honest**: Write openly and honestly about your thoughts and feelings. Don't censor yourself—this is for your eyes only.

- **Review past entries**: Periodically review what you've written. This can provide valuable insights and show how you've grown over time.

Mindfulness

Mindfulness is a practice that involves staying present and fully engaging with the current moment. It encourages you to pay attention to your thoughts, feelings, and sensations without judgment. By being mindful, you can gain a better understanding of yourself and your reactions, which can enhance your self-awareness and overall well-being.

Engaging in mindfulness can help:

- reduce stress

- improve your focus

- promote emotional regulation

It is a skill that can be cultivated through various techniques like meditation, deep breathing, and yoga. By incorporating mindfulness into your daily life, you can develop a greater sense of clarity, compassion, and resilience.

Simple Mindfulness Practices

- **Mindful breathing**: Focus on your breath. Pay attention to the sensation of air entering and leaving your body. This practice helps calm your mind and center your thoughts.

- **Body scan**: Slowly move your attention through different parts of your body, noticing any tension or sensations. This can help you become more aware of how stress or emotions manifest physically.

- **Mindful observation**: Choose an object and study it closely. Notice its details, colors, and textures. This practice trains your mind to focus and become more aware of your surroundings.

Incorporating Mindfulness Into Daily Life

- **Start small**: Begin with a few minutes of mindfulness practice daily. Gradually increase the time as you become more comfortable.

- **Use everyday moments**: Practice mindfulness during activities like eating, walking, or washing dishes. Being present in these moments can help you build mindfulness into your daily life.

Feedback

Feedback is an invaluable tool for self-improvement. Seeking input from others can give you perspectives that may otherwise not be evident. Constructive feedback can help you to recognize your strengths and pinpoint areas for growth. So, be bold and ask for feedback from people you trust, and be specific about what you want feedback on to get the most useful insights.

Embracing the feedback that you receive as a means of improvement can lead to enhanced skills, better relationships, and increased performance. Being open to feedback demonstrates your willingness to learn and grow. Remembering the value of feedback can guide you toward continual self-reflection and advancement, ultimately contributing to your well-being and success. With that said, choose to be open and approach feedback with an open mind. Listen without getting defensive, and try understanding the other person's perspective.

It is also important to spend time reflecting on the feedback that you have received. Are there any patterns that you notice? Does any of this feedback align with your own self-perceptions? Once you have done this, use the feedback to make positive changes, remembering that setting goals based on the feedback can help you grow and improve.

Further Resources

Recommended Books

1. ***The Power of Now* by Eckhart Tolle:** This book is a fantastic guide to living in the present moment and

understanding the importance of mindfulness in everyday life. Tolle offers practical advice on how to let go of past regrets and future anxieties and focus on the here and now.

2. ***Emotional Intelligence* by Daniel Goleman:** Goleman's book dives deep into EI and how it affects our relationships and success. It's a great resource for understanding how self-awareness and managing your emotions can lead to better outcomes in life.

3. ***Radical Acceptance* by Tara Brach:** In this book, Brach explores how embracing ourselves fully, including our flaws and struggles, can lead to profound personal growth and peace. It's a powerful read for anyone looking to enhance their self-awareness and self-compassion.

Recommended Articles

1. **"How to Practice Mindfulness" by Mindful:** This article provides practical tips and techniques for incorporating mindfulness into your daily routine. It's a helpful starting point if you're new to mindfulness or looking for ways to deepen your practice.

2. **"Self-Awareness: An Antidote to the Rat Race":** This piece explains the research behind self-awareness and how it impacts our behavior and relationships. It's an informative read that helps one understand the scientific side of self-awareness.

3. **"30 Best Self-Exploration Questions, Journal Prompts, & Tools":** This guide offers comprehensive advice on how to use journaling as a tool for self-discovery. It includes tips, prompts, and strategies to help you get the most out of your journaling practice.

The additional resources mentioned above will provide valuable insights and practical tips to deepen your understanding of self-awareness and emotional management. Happy reading!

Chapter 4:

The Art of Self-Control

Self-control is one mark of a mature person; it applies to control of language, physical treatment of others, and the appetites of the body. –Joseph B. Wirthlin

As Claire's self-awareness grew, she realized another aspect of herself: She wasn't always great at controlling her reactions. While recognizing her emotions was a big step forward, it didn't necessarily prevent her from snapping when stressed or avoiding conversations she didn't want to have. Self-awareness was one thing, but self-control was a whole new challenge.

Claire noticed something in everyday moments. While driving to work, she'd get frustrated when someone cut her off. After practicing self-awareness, she realized her anger wasn't about the traffic but her stress. Claire decided to master self-control by responding in a way that served her best rather than being ruled by her emotions.

The first thing that Claire learned was that self-control was not about suppressing her feelings but the opposite. Claire found that the more she acknowledged her emotions without judgment, the easier it became to manage them. She started practicing what she called "the pause." Whenever she felt like she was about to react, she would pause, take a deep breath, and ask herself a simple question: What is really happening here?

During a busy workweek, Claire was frustrated and on the verge of losing her patience with a colleague who misunderstood her instructions. Instead of reacting angrily, she took a break, went for a walk, and returned calmer, able to respond calmly.

The benefits of self-control also started to spill into other parts of Claire's life. She noticed that she was quicker to communicate with her partner when something bothered her instead of bottling it up and then snapping later. When she felt an emotional reaction rising, she would pause, breathe, and choose her response. This simple practice started to defuse tension before it escalated.

One of the biggest changes came with her own inner critic. Claire used to be her harshest judge, beating herself up for every little mistake. But now, when that familiar voice of self-doubt crept in, she paused and asked herself if those thoughts were really helpful. Most of the time, they weren't. Instead of spiraling into negativity, she learned to redirect her focus and move on with a little more kindness toward herself.

Claire was learning that she didn't have to let her emotions control her actions. While emotions were valuable guides, she realized she was responsible for her responses. Even though Claire wasn't perfect and still had moments of reacting without thinking, she was becoming more intentional, present, and empowered. As she practiced, Claire felt like she was mastering the art of living and self-control—responding to life calmly rather than just reacting to it.

Mastering the Pause

The art of self-control is your key to staying steady and focused, even when life throws curveballs your way. It is about harnessing the power to manage your thoughts, emotions, and reactions so that you can make thoughtful decisions rather than acting on impulse. Self-control is like a superpower that helps you remain calm and composed during stressful situations, handle your emotions more effectively, and stay on track with your goals.

When you are self-controlled, you do not just react to life's challenges; you are in total charge of how you respond. This ability to pause and think before acting can prevent you from making impulsive decisions that you might later regret. It helps you deal with stress and anxiety in a healthier way, making it easier to maintain your balance and focus.

Self-control also plays an important role in overcoming procrastination. By breaking down tasks into manageable steps and staying committed to your goals, you can achieve more and feel less overwhelmed.

Self-Control: Importance in Daily Life

You can think of self-control as a muscle that grows stronger with practice. The more you exercise it, the better you'll be able to handle life's ups and downs. Self-control is the ability to manage your impulses, emotions, and behaviors in a way that aligns with your long-term goals and values. It is about resisting immediate temptations or distractions and making choices that support your overall well-being.

In daily life, self-control is important because it helps you stay focused on what truly matters. Whether you are trying to stick to a budget, maintain a healthy lifestyle, or achieve personal and professional, goals, self-control allows you to make decisions that lead to better outcomes and avoid actions that could lead to regret.

Self-Control, Stress, and Anxiety

Self-control plays a significant role in how you handle stress and anxiety. When you have strong self-control, you can better manage stress by maintaining a calm and rational perspective, even in challenging situations. This means you can pause, assess your options, and respond in a measured way rather than reacting impulsively.

On the other side, stress and anxiety can test your self-control. High levels of stress and anxiety can make it harder to stay focused and resist temptations, leading to impulsive decisions or unhealthy coping mechanisms.

By improving your self-control, you can better manage these emotions, reduce their impact, and navigate life's pressures more easily. Developing self-control helps create a buffer against the negative effects of stress and anxiety, promoting a more balanced and resilient approach to life.

Understanding Stress and Anxiety

Stress is a natural response to demands or challenges, and it comes in two main forms: acute and chronic. Understanding these types of stress can help in developing appropriate coping strategies to manage them effectively.

- **Acute stress:** This is short-term stress that occurs in response to immediate, specific situations, like preparing for a big presentation or dealing with a sudden emergency. It is typically temporary and subsides once the situation is resolved.

- **Chronic stress:** This is long-term stress resulting from ongoing pressures and difficulties, like persistent work problems, financial troubles, or relationship conflicts. Chronic stress can build up over time and may lead to more serious health issues if not managed properly.

On the other hand, anxiety is a persistent state of worry or fear that often occurs without a clear, immediate cause. While similar to stress in its impact, anxiety is more about an ongoing feeling of unease and apprehension.

- **Differences from stress:** Stress is usually linked to a specific external situation, while anxiety is more about internal fears and worries. Stress tends to be short-term and situation-specific, whereas anxiety can be more pervasive and long-lasting.

- **Similarities to stress:** Both stress and anxiety can cause physical symptoms like increased heart rate and muscle tension, and they can impact your emotional well-being, leading to feelings of overwhelm and difficulty concentrating.

Common Stress and Anxiety Triggers

Let's have a look at what can trigger stress and anxiety:

Work-Related Pressures

Work-related pressures are a major source of stress and anxiety for many people. Examples of this can include:

- tight deadlines
- heavy workloads
- job security concerns
- constant demand to meet expectations
- increasing responsibilities

Financial Concerns

Financial issues are another common trigger. Problems like:

- budgeting difficulties
- debt
- financial instability
- worrying about paying bills
- concerns about managing expenses
- worrying about saving for future goals

Relationship Issues

Relationships can be rewarding, but they can also contribute to stress and anxiety. While no-one thrives in environments where there are conflict, sometimes it is unavoidable and unfortunately conflicts within family, friends, or partners can also be significant stressors.

Disagreements, misunderstandings, or emotional strain in relationships can lead to feelings of frustration and anxiety. Additionally, navigating complex dynamics and trying to resolve conflicts can be emotionally taxing.

Major Life Changes

Major life events, like moving to a new home, starting a new job, or experiencing significant changes in your personal life, can be sources of stress and anxiety. Even positive changes, like a promotion or new relationship, can bring about stress as you adjust to new circumstances and responsibilities.

Understanding and recognizing these triggers is the initial step in effectively managing stress and anxiety. By understanding the causes of your stress, you can develop strategies to address and reduce the challenges that come with them.

Stress and anxiety affect both your body and mind. Physiologically, they can lead to symptoms like headaches, fatigue, high blood pressure, and digestive issues. Psychologically, they can cause feelings of irritability, trouble focusing, and mood swings. Chronic exposure to stress and anxiety can contribute to more serious health conditions, like cardiovascular disease and mental health disorders.

Stress and Anxiety Management Techniques

Mindfulness

Mindfulness helps reduce stress by encouraging you to focus on the present moment rather than worrying about past events or future concerns. By practicing mindfulness, you can break the cycle of automatic stress responses and develop a more balanced perspective, leading to reduced stress levels and improved emotional well-being.

Step-by-Step Guide to Basic Mindfulness:

1. **Find a quiet space:** Sit or lie down in a comfortable position in a quiet environment.

2. **Focus on your breath:** Close your eyes and focus on your breathing. Notice the sensation of the air entering and leaving your body.

3. **Observe without judgment:** As thoughts come to mind, observe them without judgment and gently bring your focus back to your breath.

4. **Practice regularly:** Start with just a few minutes each day and gradually increase as you become more comfortable with the practice.

Breathing Exercises

Deep breathing helps calm your nervous system and reduce stress by activating the body's relaxation response. Focusing on your breath can lower your heart rate and promote a sense of calm.

Techniques that you can try to include:

- **4-7-8 Breathing:** Inhale through your nose for 4 seconds, hold your breath for 7 seconds, and exhale completely through your mouth for 8 seconds. Repeat this cycle a few times to help calm your mind.

- **Box Breathing:** Inhale through your nose for 4 seconds, hold for 4 seconds, exhale through your mouth for 4 seconds, and hold again for 4 seconds. Repeat several times to promote relaxation.

Physical Activity

Exercise is a powerful stress reliever. It helps release endorphins, which are natural mood lifters, and improves physical health, making you better equipped to handle stress.

Daily Exercises and Their Benefits:

- **Walking:** A brisk 30-minute walk can boost your mood and energy levels while providing a break from daily stressors.

- **Stretching:** Gentle stretching helps relieve muscle tension and improve flexibility, reducing physical stress.

- **Yoga:** Combining movement with mindfulness, yoga helps improve flexibility, strength, and mental clarity.

Time Management

Effective time management helps you stay organized and reduces the stress of feeling overwhelmed by tasks. By prioritizing and planning, you can manage your workload more efficiently.

Tips for Effective Time Management:

- **Create a to-do list:** Write down tasks and prioritize them based on deadlines and importance.

- **Break tasks into smaller steps:** Divide larger projects into manageable steps to make them less overwhelming.

- **Use time blocks:** Allocate specific times for each task and avoid multitasking to maintain focus and productivity.

Positive Self-Talk

Positive self-talk involves replacing negative or self-critical thoughts with affirmations that reinforce your strengths and capabilities. This practice helps shift your mindset towards a more optimistic and resilient outlook.

Examples of Stress-Reducing Affirmations:

- "I am in control of my thoughts and feelings."

- "I can handle any challenge that comes my way."

- "I am calm, focused, and centered."

By incorporating these techniques into your routine, you can manage stress and anxiety more effectively, leading to a more balanced and peaceful life.

Recognizing and Understanding Your Emotional Triggers

Understanding what triggers your emotional responses is the first step in managing them effectively. Emotional triggers are specific events, situations, or interactions that cause strong emotional reactions, like anger, sadness, or anxiety. By identifying these triggers, you can start recognizing patterns in your emotional responses and gain insight into why you react the way you do. This awareness allows you to prepare for or avoid situations that typically lead to negative emotions and helps you develop strategies to handle them better when they arise.

Techniques for Regulating Emotions in Stressful Situations

1. **Pause and breathe:** When you feel a strong emotion building up, take a moment to pause and focus on your breath. Deep breathing can help calm your nervous system and create a space for you to respond more thoughtfully.

2. **Practice mindfulness:** Stay present and observe your emotions without judgment. Acknowledge what you're feeling and why, then choose a constructive way to address it. Mindfulness helps you gain clarity and manage your emotions more effectively.

3. **Use cognitive reframing:** Change how you perceive a stressful situation by shifting your perspective. Instead of viewing challenges as threats, try to see them as opportunities for growth or learning.

4. **Express emotions constructively:** Find healthy ways to express your emotions, like talking to a trusted friend, journaling, or engaging in creative activities. Expressing yourself can help release pent-up feelings and provide relief.

The Role of Emotional Intelligence in Managing Stress and Anxiety

Emotional intelligence (EI) involves recognizing, understanding, and managing your own emotions, as well as empathizing with others. It plays a crucial role in handling stress and anxiety by enabling you to:

- understand your emotional state and how it affects your behavior and decisions

- manage your emotions in a healthy way, preventing them from overwhelming you or leading to impulsive actions

- recognize and respond to the emotions of others, which can improve relationships and reduce interpersonal stress

- communicate effectively and resolve conflicts in a constructive manner, helping to alleviate stress in social and professional settings

Overcoming Procrastination

Some do not realize it, but procrastination can lead to increased stress. When you delay tasks, deadlines loom larger, and you may experience heightened anxiety about completing them on time. This can create a cycle where the stress of looming deadlines makes it even harder to get started, leading to more procrastination. Understanding this link helps you recognize that overcoming procrastination is about improving productivity, reducing stress, and improving your well-being.

You can overcome procrastination by implementing certain strategies, including:

1. **Breaking tasks into smaller steps.** Large tasks can feel overwhelming and lead to procrastination. Breaking them down into smaller, manageable steps makes them feel more achievable and less intimidating. For example, instead of "write report," break it into "outline sections," "research topic," and "draft introduction." Completing each small step provides a sense of accomplishment and keeps you moving forward.

2. **Setting realistic goals and deadlines.** Set clear, realistic goals and deadlines to provide structure and direction. Make sure

your goals are specific, measurable, and attainable. Instead of "finish project," set a goal like "complete the first draft by Friday." Having well-defined deadlines helps you stay focused and creates a sense of urgency without being overwhelming.

3. **Using the pomodoro technique.** The Pomodoro Technique is a time management method that involves working in short, focused intervals, typically 25 minutes, followed by a five-minute break. After four intervals, take a longer break. This technique helps maintain focus and productivity by breaking work into manageable chunks and providing regular breaks to avoid burnout.

4. **The importance of self-compassion in avoiding procrastination.** Being kind to yourself is crucial when overcoming procrastination. Understand that everyone procrastinates at times, and beating yourself up only adds to stress and discouragement. Practice self-compassion by acknowledging your challenges, celebrating small victories, and focusing on progress rather than perfection. This positive approach helps maintain motivation and reduces the negative emotions that can fuel procrastination.

Exercise: Self-Control Development

This exercise aims to enhance your self-control, an essential component of emotional intelligence, by helping you recognize triggers, implement strategies to manage impulses, and reflect on your progress.

You will need:

- notebook or digital document for journaling
- pen or typing device

- timer or timer app

Instructions:

Step 1: Identify Your Triggers

- **Set aside time for reflection:** Dedicate 10–15 minutes to think about situations in your life where you struggle with self-control. This could include emotional eating, procrastination, impulsive spending, or reacting defensively in conflict.

- **List your triggers:** Write down specific scenarios or triggers that lead to impulsive behavior. For example, "I tend to snack mindlessly in front of the TV" or "I often procrastinate when I feel overwhelmed by tasks.

Step 2: Set Clear Goals

- **Define specific goals:** For each trigger that you have identified, set a clear and achievable goal for improvement. For example, "I will limit my TV snacking to one healthy snack per episode" or "I will break tasks into smaller steps and tackle them one at a time."

- **Make it measurable:** Ensure your goals are measurable. Instead of "I want to be more productive," specify "I will work for 25 minutes and then take a five-minute break."

Step 3: Develop Strategies

Create action plans: For each trigger and goal, develop a specific action plan. For example:

- **Snacking:** Prepare healthy snacks in advance and keep them portioned. Avoid keeping unhealthy snacks at home.

- **Procrastination:** Use the Pomodoro Technique (25 minutes of focused work followed by a five-minute break).

- **Emotional reactions:** Use deep breathing or mindfulness should be practiced to pause before responding to stressful situations.

Step 4: Implement the Strategies

- **Practice daily:** Begin implementing your action plans daily, focusing on one or two strategies at a time to avoid overwhelm.

- **Use reminders:** Set reminders on your phone or use sticky notes in prominent places to reinforce your goals and strategies.

Step 5: Reflect and Analyze

- **Weekly reflection:** At the end of each week, take 15–20 minutes to reflect on your experiences. Write down: What strategies worked well and helped you maintain self-control? What challenges did you face, and how did you handle them? Were there situations where you reverted to old habits? If so, what triggered that response?

- **Adjust your goals**: Based on your reflections, adjust your goals or strategies as needed. Don't be afraid to modify your approach if something isn't working.

Step 6: Celebrate your Progress

- **Acknowledge your victories:** Celebrate every small win and acknowledge your progress. You could do this through journaling, treating yourself to a small reward, or sharing your achievements with a friend.

- **Visualize your success:** Spend a few moments each week visualizing yourself successfully navigating situations where you previously struggled with self-control. Imagine how you will feel and the positive impact it will have on your emotional well-being.

Step 7: Seek Support

- **Engage with others:** Share your goals with a trusted friend or family member who can hold you accountable. Seek their support as you navigate challenges and celebrate your achievements together.

- **Join a group:** Consider joining a support group or program focused on developing self-control or emotional intelligence. Sharing experiences and getting encouragement from others can be incredibly beneficial.

Additional Tips

- Remember to be patient with yourself; developing self-control takes time and persistent effort.

- Take time to reflect on improved self-control's broader impact on your emotional intelligence and relationships.

- Regularly revisit and revise your goals and strategies, ensuring they remain relevant to your evolving journey.

By working on this exercise regularly, you'll build stronger self-control, which will help you become more aware of your emotions and respond better in different situations. This journey is all about you, and your dedication to improving will lead to personal growth and greater emotional intelligence. Embrace the process, and you'll see positive changes in your life.

Interactive Element: Stress Management Exercise

Guided Exercise: Identifying Stress Triggers and Creating a Personalized Stress Management Plan

1. Identifying your stress triggers.

Begin by reflecting on situations or events that commonly lead to stress in your life. Use the following prompts to help identify your stress triggers:

- **Situations:** What specific situations tend to make you feel stressed? (e.g., work deadlines, family conflicts.)

- **People:** Are there certain people who trigger stress for you? (e.g., demanding boss, argumentative friends.)

- **Places:** Do particular environments contribute to your stress? (e.g., crowded spaces, noisy areas.)

- **Thoughts:** Are there recurring thoughts or worries that increase your stress levels? (e.g., fear of failure, self-doubt.)

Situations	People	Places	Thoughts

2. Creating a personalized stress management plan.

Once you've identified your stress triggers, create a plan tailored to your needs:

- **List your top stress triggers:** Write down the main situations, people, or thoughts that cause stress.

- **Develop coping strategies:** For each trigger, note down specific strategies to manage your stress. Consider techniques like mindfulness, deep breathing, or physical activity.

- **Set actionable goals:** Define clear, achievable goals for implementing your stress management strategies. For example, "Practice deep breathing for five minutes daily" or "Schedule weekly exercise sessions."

Reflection Questions

Reflect on the specific situations, people, or thoughts that typically cause you stress. Consider both daily occurrences and more significant events.

How do you usually respond to stress and anxiety? Think about your typical reactions when you experience stress or anxiety. Do you become irritable, withdraw from others, or seek unhealthy coping mechanisms?

Reflect on the strategies or techniques you've used to cope with stress in the past. Have you found mindfulness, physical activity, or time management helpful? Consider what has worked well for you and any adjustments you might need to make to improve your stress management practices.

Reflect on your journey with self-control and stress management. Consider how your ability to handle stress has evolved and how you want to implement these techniques. Reflect on the positive changes you've experienced and the areas where you want to continue growing.

Chapter 5:

Building Resilience

Enthusiasm is common, endurance is rare. –Angela Duckworth

After Claire's experience facing her inner shadows, she realized something important: Life was not just about avoiding pain or seeking comfort. It was about growing through challenges, even when they felt overwhelming. She was doing the inner work she needed to do to connect with her inner child, and now it was time for her to build the resilience she needed to keep moving forward.

Claire had set her intentions on strengthening her resilience. She knew that she would have to take things one step at a time and that she should not expect an overnight transformation, but she was committed to the journey.

First, Claire made a habit of practicing mindfulness. She began to notice the subtle ways that stress crept into her life, the tightness in her chest when she felt overwhelmed, and the negative thoughts that would spiral out of control when things did not go as planned. But instead of letting those feelings overtake her, she learned to pause. She would sit with her emotions, breathe through them, and remind herself that this moment, however challenging, would pass.

As Claire practiced mindfulness, she noticed that she could better manage difficult situations. When she felt like life was too much for her to handle, instead of reacting impulsively or feeling paralyzed, she found that she could create space between her emotions and her actions. This space allowed her to choose responses that were aligned with her values rather than acting out of fear or frustration.

Claire also made it a point to seek connection with others. For years, she had tried to handle everything on her own, believing that asking for help was a sign of weakness. But as she started opening up and sharing her struggles with trusted friends, she found that vulnerability was a source of strength. Her friends offered support and understanding, and in return, she felt more grounded and connected. This sense of belonging gave her the courage to face challenges without feeling like she had to do it all alone.

Another critical step in building resilience was how Claire reframed her mindset. She started to view setbacks not as failures but as opportunities for growth. Whenever something did not go as planned, she asked herself, "What can I learn from this?" Over time, this simple question shifted her relationship with adversity. Instead of feeling defeated, she became curious and more open to finding solutions.

As Claire's resilience grew, so did the positive benefits in her life. She noticed that she bounced back from difficult situations quicker. Things that used to cause her anxiety or frustration no longer had the same power over her. She had a greater sense of emotional stability, and even on tough days, she trusted that she had the inner strength to handle whatever came her way.

Claire's relationships also deepened. By practicing vulnerability and asking for help when she needed it, she was able to build stronger relationships with those around her. Her friends and family appreciated her honesty and felt closer to her. The walls that she had once built out of fear of rejection began to crumble and were replaced with trust and mutual support.

One of the most profound benefits, was how resilient Claire was becoming in pursuing her passions. In the past, she would abandon projects at the first sign of difficulty because she feared she was incapable or deserving of success. Now, with her newfound resilient mindset, she viewed challenges as part of the process. Whether it was creating art, writing, or starting new ventures, Claire showed up with a newfound determination. She embraced the messy middle, the part of her journey where things felt uncertain, knowing that growth often came from those very moments.

With each challenge she faced, Claire discovered that she was not just surviving; she was thriving. The resilience she had cultivated became a source of empowerment, reminding her that no matter what life threw her way, she had the strength to rise again and again.

Resilience Matters

Resilience is what empowers you to bounce back from inevitable setbacks. Whether it is a personal loss, a professional failure, or a challenging situation, resilience allows you to recover and keep moving forward. The importance of resilience lies in its ability to help you adapt to change, manage stress, and maintain your well-being during tough times. It is not just about surviving difficulties but thriving in adversity.

Effective strategies play a key role in building resilience. Even when things are unplanned, staying positive helps you to maintain a healthy mindset. Learning from mistakes instead of dwelling on them allows you to grow and improve. Persistence, or the determination to keep going despite obstacles, is another critical aspect of resilience. These strategies help you navigate challenges and contribute to your personal growth.

When you develop resilience, you transform challenges into opportunities for self-improvement. Each setback becomes a lesson, and every difficulty faced adds to your strength and wisdom. Over time, these experiences shape you into a more confident, capable person.

You will achieve long-term personal and professional success when you bounce back and keep moving forward. Combined with effective strategies, resilience turns obstacles into stepping stones toward a brighter future so that you can grow and achieve all your goals in life.

Growth Mindset Versus a Fixed Mindset

Perhaps you have heard of a growth mindset and a fixed mindset, but you are not completely sure what they really are. Before you read any further, let's look at what each of them is.

A growth mindset is the belief that you can improve your abilities, intelligence, and skills through effort, learning, and persistence. On the other hand, a fixed mindset is the belief that your abilities and intelligence are set in stone, meaning that you either have them or you do not. In short, a growth mindset is believing that you can improve, while a fixed mindset believes that you are stuck with what you have got.

Below are some examples illustrating the difference between a growth and a fixed mindset. These examples highlight how a fixed mindset limits potential by seeing abilities as static, while a growth mindset encourages learning, resilience, and continuous development.

Situation	Fixed Mindset	Growth Mindset
Approach to challenges	"I'm not good at math, so I avoid it whenever possible." This person believes their math ability is fixed and doesn't see the value in trying to improve.	"Math is challenging for me, but I can improve with practice. I'll take extra time to study and seek help if needed." This person sees math as a skill that can be developed and is willing to try to improve.
Response to failure	"I failed the exam, which means I'm just not smart enough." This perspective sees failure as a reflection of their innate ability.	"I failed the exam, but this is an opportunity to learn. I'll review my mistakes and study more to do better next time."

	feels discouraged.	This approach views failure as a chance to learn and grow rather than a definitive measure of their abilities.
Feedback from others	"That feedback is harsh. They don't appreciate my talents, so I don't need to listen to it." This person feels threatened by criticism and sees it as a personal attack on their abilities.	"The feedback is tough, but it's valuable. I'll use it to improve my skills and performance." This person views feedback as a tool for improvement and is open to making changes based on it.
Effort and persistence	"I tried hard, but I'm still not good at this. I guess it's just not for me." This attitude gives up easily when results don't come quickly, believing effort won't lead to improvement.	"I may not be good at this yet, but with continued effort and practice, I can get better." This attitude embraces effort and persistence, understanding that improvement comes with time and practice.

A growth mindset is a powerful tool for personal and professional development. Embracing a growth mindset brings with it numerous benefits and encourages you to take on challenges confidently, knowing that effort will lead to improvement. This mindset helps you to adapt and thrive in an ever-changing world.

Some benefits of having a growth mindset include:

- increased resilience

- enhanced learning and skill development

- better problem-solving skills

- improved achievements and performance

- being more open to feedback

- increased motivation and engagement

The good news is that if you have a fixed mindset, you can develop a growth mindset. Developing a growth mindset is all about changing how you think about challenges, effort, and learning. Over time, as you practice certain habits, your mindset can shift from fixed to growth, helping you face new challenges more confidently.

Here are a few ways in which you can start to develop a growth mindset:

- **Challenge the idea of "natural talent":** Viewing success as a product of effort rather than innate ability can help keep you motivated to keep learning.

- **Embrace challenges:** Instead of avoiding difficult tasks, view them as opportunities to grow and learn.

- **Learn from failure:** Rather than seeing failure as the end, treat it as a stepping stone to improvement. Ask yourself, "What can I learn from this?"

- **Celebrate effort:** Focus on the process and the effort that you are putting in, not just the result. This shifts the focus from being "good at something" to "get better."

- **Replace negative self-talk:** Instead of saying, "I cannot do this," try "I cannot do this yet." That simple shift in language can remind you that progress is possible.

- **Seek feedback:** Be open to constructive criticism, which can help you see where you can grow and improve.

- **Visualize growth:** Imagine yourself learning and improving over time. Visualizing success and growth can help strengthen the belief that you can change.

- **Practice self-compassion:** Be kind to yourself when you make mistakes. Everyone has setbacks, but how you respond to them is key. Treat yourself with the same patience and encouragement you would give a friend.

- **Surround yourself with growth-oriented people:** Spend time with people who value learning and growth. Positive influences can help reinforce a growth mindset and challenge you to think in new ways.

Maintaining Emotional Balance

Emotional balance is the ability to manage and respond to your emotions in a healthy and constructive way. It's about finding stability amidst the ups and downs of life so that your emotions don't overwhelm you or dictate your actions.

There is a strong connection between having a growth mindset and maintaining emotional balance while building resilience. Let's have a look at how they tie together:

- **A growth mindset promotes resilience:** A growth mindset encourages you to see challenges, setbacks, and failures as part of the learning process, not as permanent defeat. This perspective makes you more resilient because you are more likely to bounce back from difficulties, knowing that they are opportunities for growth. Instead of getting stuck in frustration or negative emotions, you see setbacks as temporary and fixable.

  - **Emotional balance through a growth mindset:** When you adopt a growth mindset, you do not take failure or criticism as a personal attack on your abilities or self-worth. You become less emotionally reactive, more patient with yourself, and better at navigating difficult emotions. This emotional balance comes from understanding that you are in a process of constant improvement, and setbacks are not a reflection of your overall value.

- **Resilience strengthens emotional balance:** Building resilience involves learning how to cope with stress, bounce back from difficulties, and stay flexible through tough times. When you build resilience through a growth mindset, it reinforces your emotional balance because you are able to handle emotional ups and downs better. Resilience helps you to stay grounded in difficult situations and reduces the intensity of negative emotions.

- **Viewing challenges as growth opportunities:** With a growth mindset, you naturally start to view difficult situations or emotionally charged moments as opportunities to practice emotional control and strengthen resilience. This helps you maintain a more positive emotional state, even in hard times.

- **Increased self-efficacy:** As you develop a growth mindset, you build confidence in your ability to improve and overcome challenges. This belief in yourself—known as self-efficacy—contributes to emotional balance. When you believe you can handle challenges, you feel less overwhelmed, less anxious, and more in control of your emotions, making it easier to stay resilient.

Maintaining emotional balance involves self-awareness, resilience, and the ability to navigate stress and challenges with a calm and centered approach. The first step in maintaining emotional balance is recognizing your emotional responses to setbacks. Understanding how you react emotionally—whether it's frustration, sadness, or anger—can help you manage these feelings more effectively. By identifying your emotions, you can take control of your reactions instead of letting them control you.

By recognizing your emotional responses and using these techniques to regulate them, you can build resilience and maintain emotional balance, even in life's challenges. Below are several techniques you can use to regulate your emotions effectively. These techniques can be integrated into your daily routine for improved emotional resilience and regulation.

Mindfulness & Meditation

- Practice mindfulness: Focus on the present moment without judgment, observing your thoughts and feelings.

- Breathing exercises: Deep, slow breathing can help calm your nervous system and reduce stress.

- Body scan meditation: Focus on how each part of your body feels, releasing tension.

Cognitive Reframing

- Challenge negative thoughts: Identify irrational or overly negative thoughts and replace them with more balanced perspectives.

- Perspective-taking: Try to see a situation from different angles, which can reduce emotional intensity.

Emotional Labeling

- Name the emotion: Simply labeling what you're feeling ("I'm angry," "I'm anxious") can help reduce the emotion's power over you.

- Understand triggers: Recognizing what situations or people trigger certain emotions can help you prepare and manage your response better.

Self-Compassion

- Be kind to yourself: Treat yourself with the same compassion you would offer a friend who is going through a tough time.

- Avoid self-criticism: Replace critical thoughts with encouraging or neutral ones.

Physical Regulation

- Exercise: Physical activity releases endorphins that can improve your mood.

- Sleep & nutrition: Prioritize rest and healthy eating, which contribute to emotional balance.

Progressive Muscle Relaxation

- Tense and release muscles: Go through each part of your body, tensing muscles for a few seconds, then relaxing. This helps reduce physical stress linked to emotions.

Journaling

- Write about your feelings: Writing out your emotions can give you clarity and help you process intense feelings.

- Gratitude journal: Focus on positive aspects of your life, which can shift your emotional state.

Time-Out & Distraction

- Take a break: Step away from the situation to calm down before reacting.

- Engage in a hobby or activity: Sometimes, distracting yourself with something enjoyable can diffuse emotional tension.

Seek Social Support

- Talk to someone: Sharing your emotions with a trusted friend or family member can provide relief and a new perspective.

- Empathy practice: Listen to others' experiences to understand how they cope with similar emotions.

Emotional Regulation Strategies

- Opposite action: When an emotion feels overwhelming, do the opposite action of what the emotion is urging you to do. For example, if you're angry, respond with calmness or kindness.

- TIP skills (Temperature, Intense exercise, Paced breathing, Progressive relaxation): These help calm the body and emotions when they become overwhelming.

Further Resources: Recommended Books and Articles on Resilience

Below are resources that will provide valuable insights and practical advice for building resilience and adopting a growth mindset, helping you navigate life's challenges confidently and gracefully.

Books

- ***Mindset: The New Psychology of Success* by Carol S. Dweck:** This book explores the concept of a growth mindset and how it can transform your life. Carol Dweck, a leading psychologist, delves into the power of believing that our abilities can be developed through dedication and hard work.

- ***Resilient: How to Grow an Unshakable Core of Calm, Strength, and Happiness* by Rick Hanson:** Rick Hanson provides practical strategies for building resilience and cultivating an inner strength to withstand life's challenges. This book guides the development of a deep sense of well-being and emotional balance.

Articles

- **"Building Your Resilience"**: This article delves into the psychological aspects of resilience, offering insights into the science behind it and practical tips for developing this essential skill. It's a great read for understanding how resilience works and how you can build it.

- **"The Benefits of Cultivating a Growth Mindset"**: This article provides a detailed exploration of the growth mindset, offers strategies to develop it, and highlights the benefits of adopting this approach to challenges. It's a useful resource for anyone looking to deepen their understanding of a growth mindset.

Chapter 6:

Motivation and Goal Setting

You are never too old to set another goal or to dream a new dream. –Les Brown

As Claire continued to work on building her emotional intelligence, she realized something was missing. She realized that she felt disconnected from her goals and unsure of her motivations. To understand herself better, she began journaling regularly with a new focus.

Claire started journaling her thoughts every morning, identifying what excited her, what drained her, and where she procrastinated. She questioned her true desires and gradually realized that many of her goals were based on others' expectations rather than hers. This breakthrough made her aware of how often she sought approval or feared failure rather than following her genuine sense of purpose.

This self-awareness helped Claire set more meaningful goals by breaking them into smaller steps, focusing on progress over perfection. She prioritized creative projects, relationships, and emotional well-being, allowing herself time to grow without strict deadlines because she knew the journey was as important as the destination.

Claire focused on understanding her emotions while working towards her goals, realizing that her feelings provided clues to her motivations, which helped her navigate her path forward. For example, when feeling anxious or frustrated, she would pause and reflect, asking herself, "What is this emotion trying to tell me? Do I need to address something? Am I avoiding a fear?"

Claire soon realized that setting goals out of genuine interest, like writing a heartfelt story or spending time in nature, energized her. Her emotions became a compass, guiding her toward what was most meaningful and away from pursuits that left her feeling empty.

After aligning her goals with her inner motivations, Claire's life changed positively. She felt more grounded and had a stronger sense of direction, engaging in fulfilling activities and finding the strength to persevere through tough times.

Claire's increased emotional intelligence strengthened her relationships, making her more empathetic and supportive. She found a strong link between motivation, emotions, and resilience, setting meaningful goals that led to a more purposeful life focused on self-awareness and genuine connections that honored her true self.

The Connection Between Emotional Intelligence, Motivations, and Your Goals

Motivation and goal-setting are deeply connected to emotional intelligence (EI) because they both deal with understanding and managing your emotions in a way that supports personal growth. EI is all about recognizing your own emotions, understanding what drives them, and using that knowledge to thrive in life.

Emotional intelligence gives you the tools that you need to set goals that are meaningful, stay motivated in a healthy way, and manage the emotions that arise on your journey to success. It turns goals from something that you "have to do" into something that genuinely fulfills you and pushes you to grow emotionally.

Now, let's have a closer look at how this important connection works:

Understanding Your Motivations

Emotional intelligence helps you to identify why you feel motivated or unmotivated in different situations. Are you driven by fear, excitement, or personal growth? Being emotionally intelligent allows you to recognize these feelings and align your motivations with what genuinely matters to you, rather than reacting based on short-term impulses.

For example, if you know that stress makes you procrastinate, EI can help you manage stress and refocus on why your goal matters, which can reignite your motivation.

Setting Goals With Emotional Awareness

Goal-setting isn't just about achieving external success; it is also about emotional satisfaction. When you use emotional intelligence (EI) to set your goals, you are more likely to choose ones that align with your values, fulfill your emotional needs, and bring long-term happiness rather than goals that might bring short-term wins but leave you feeling empty.

Example: Instead of setting a goal to make more money, if you have strong emotional intelligence, you might set a goal to find work that is meaningful and aligns with your passions. This way, your motivation will remain strong because the goal satisfies them emotionally as well.

Managing Your Emotions on the Path to Goals

Emotional intelligence can help you handle the ups and downs that life might throw your way on the way to achieving your goals. You might face setbacks, frustrations, and challenges, but with strong emotional intelligence, you can manage those emotions without giving up or getting too discouraged. It teaches you resilience and helps you to stay focused on your goals.

For example, if you feel discouraged because a project is not going as planned, EI can help you pause, reassess, and stay calm rather than give up out of frustration.

Self-Motivation and Emotional Regulation

Emotional intelligence also involves self-motivation, which is the ability to push yourself to take action even when you do not feel like it. It is about regulating your emotions so that you do not let negative feelings like fear or doubt stop you from moving forward.

For example, if you are feeling anxious about a big presentation, EI helps you manage that anxiety by focusing on your preparation and the positive outcome you are working toward.

Identifying Your Motivations: Understanding Your "Why"

In life, motivation drives every success, fuels your passions, and pushes you to achieve your goals. Without it, even the most talented people can get stuck in a place where they are not moving forward and achieving anything.

However, motivation alone isn't enough; you need a clear direction and a plan to guide you. That's where goal setting comes in. Setting goals transforms motivation into a superpower where you can take intentional, actionable steps and break your dreams down into manageable tasks. Motivation with EI and effective goal-setting can transform your aspirations into reality and ensure continuous growth.

At the heart of every goal in life lies a deeper reason: your personal "why" that drives you to achieve it. Understanding this "why" gives you clarity and purpose, guiding your decisions and actions. Motivations can vary greatly between different people and reflect their unique experiences, values, and aspirations; for example:

- personal growth
- financial security
- making a difference
- creative expression

Understanding your unique motivations allows you to set goals that resonate with your authentic self, leading to a more fulfilling and purpose-driven life. When you connect with your motivations, you can set meaningful goals that align with your values.

Your "why" can shape your approach to challenges and strategies and positively influence your life direction. Whether you are driven by personal growth, professional success, or making a positive impact, finding your "why" ensures your goals are both achievable and fulfilling.

Discovering Your Motivations and Goals

By using emotional intelligence to explore your feelings, values, interests, and past experiences, you can better understand what truly motivates you. This understanding can lead to more fulfilling decision-making and help you align your actions with what brings you genuine satisfaction and happiness in life.

Here is a step-by-step guide that can help you understand why you do things and what drives you.

Step 1: Self-Awareness

- **Recognize your emotions:** Start by paying attention to your feelings in different situations. Journaling can help you to note your emotional responses in various activities and decisions.

- **Identify your triggers:** Notice what situations or experiences trigger specific emotions. Are there any patterns? For example, do you feel excited when helping others or anxious when you face challenges?

Step 2: Reflect on Your Values

- **List your core values:** Think about what matters most to you, for example, your family, career, success, creativity, helping others, etc. These values often drive your motivations.

- **Align your actions with values:** Ask yourself if your current activities and goals align with these values. If not, consider how you can adjust your focus to better reflect what truly matters to you.

Step 3: Explore Your Interests

- **Identify what you enjoy:** What activities make you feel excited or fulfilled? Take time to explore hobbies, passions, or pursuits that spark joy.

- **Ask why you enjoy them:** For each interest, reflect on what emotions or needs they satisfy. Do you enjoy them for personal growth, social connection, or creative expression?

Step 4: Learn From the Past

- **Analyze your past decisions:** Reflect on important choices that you have made. What motivated you at the time? Did those motivations lead to satisfaction or regret?

- **Learn from the outcomes:** Consider how your emotions played a role in those decisions. Understanding past motivations can help clarify your current desires.

Step 5: Practice Active Listening

- **Listen to your inner voice:** Tune in your thoughts and feelings when you need to make decisions. What does your intuition tell you about your motivations?

- **Seek feedback:** Talk to trusted friends or mentions, as they may offer insights about your behaviors and motivations that you might not see.

Step 6: Set Intentions

- **Define clear goals:** Once you understand your motivations, set clear goals that resonate with them. Ensure that your goals reflect what you genuinely want to achieve rather than what others expect of you.

- **Monitor your progress:** Regularly check in with yourself to see if your actions are aligned with your motivations. Remember to adjust your goals as needed so that you stay true to your emotional needs.

Step 7: Empathy Matters

- **Understand other's motivations:** Observing how others navigate their motivations can give you insight into your own. Empathy helps you to recognize that different experiences can shape people's motivations.

- **Relate to shared experiences:** Engaging with others can help you to reflect on your motivations by highlighting common emotional experiences.

Step 8: Tap Into Mindfulness

- **Practice mindfulness techniques:** Techniques like meditation can help you develop a much clearer understanding of your thoughts and feelings, making it easier to identify your motivations.

- **Stay present:** Being mindful of the present moment will help you to appreciate your experiences and motivations without judgment.

Motivation Mapping Exercise

Use the space below to create a visual map that connects your goals to your motivations. Draw your goal in the center of a page, then draw lines to different motivations that support this goal. For example, if you want to write a book, your motivations might include creative expression, helping others, or achieving recognition. This map helps you see the connections between your "why" and your goals.

If find it challenging to achieve your goals, you can always reach out to friends, mentors, or professionals who can support you

Avoiding Common Pitfalls

Setting goals is one thing, but sticking to them can be challenging. Here are some common pitfalls in goal setting and strategies to overcome them. By being aware of these and implementing strategies to overcome them, you can maintain momentum and increase your chances of achieving your goals.

Pitfall	Problem	Solution
Setting vague or overly ambitious goals	Too vague or ambitious goals can lead to frustration and burnout.	Break down large goals into smaller, more specific, SMART goals. Focus on achievable milestones that build toward the larger objective.
Lack of accountability	Losing motivation and letting goals slide is easy.	Share your goals with a friend, mentor, or accountability partner. Regular check-ins can help keep you on track.
Procrastination and losing focus	Delaying action or getting distracted by other tasks can derail your progress.	Set short-term deadlines and create a schedule that includes time for goal-related activities. Use tools like reminders or habit trackers to stay focused.
Fear of failure	The fear of not achieving your goals can prevent you from taking the necessary steps.	Reframe failure as a learning opportunity. Setbacks are part of the process, and each one offers valuable

		lessons that can help you refine your approach.
Not revisiting or adjusting goals	Sticking to goals that no longer serve you can lead to frustration and a sense of being stuck.	Regularly review your goals and progress. Be open to adjusting them if your circumstances or motivations change.

The Path to Success: Staying Motivated

Maintaining motivation over the long term can be challenging, especially when the initial excitement of setting goals starts to fade. However, several techniques can help you keep your motivation high throughout your journey; for example:

- **Break down goals into smaller steps**: Large goals can feel overwhelming, making it easy to lose motivation. By breaking them down into smaller, manageable tasks, you create a sense of progress and achievement with each step completed. This keeps your motivation alive as you steadily progress to your ultimate goal.

- **Visualize success**: Regularly visualize what achieving your goal will look and feel like. Imagine the positive impact on your life and how you'll feel when you reach your destination. Visualization reinforces your commitment and keeps your motivation strong.

- **Stay connected to your "why"**: Continuously remind yourself of your underlying motivations for setting your goals in the first place. Revisiting your "why" helps to reignite your passion and keeps your focus on what truly matters.

- **Set milestones and celebrate victories**: Recognize and celebrate progress, no matter how small. Reaching milestones provides a sense of accomplishment and boosts your confidence. Celebrations can be simple, like rewarding yourself with a treat or reflecting on your progress.

- **Stay positive and practice self-compassion**: Maintaining a positive mindset is crucial for sustaining motivation. Practice self-compassion by acknowledging your efforts and being kind to yourself, especially when things are unplanned. Positive self-talk and focusing on what you've achieved rather than what's left to do can help you stay motivated.

- **Engage in positive reinforcement**: Surround yourself with supportive people who encourage you and celebrate your successes. Positive reinforcement from others can significantly boost your motivation and keep you on track.

Emotional Intelligence: Goal-Setting Worksheet

Instructions:

- Spend time thinking about your emotional strengths and areas where you want to improve. Consider how you respond to your emotions and how you interact with others.

My strengths   **Areas for improvement**

- Based on your reflection, choose 1–3 specific emotional intelligence skills to focus on. This might include self-awareness, self-regulation, empathy, social skills, or motivation.

Skill focus

- Make your goals specific, measurable, achievable, relevant, and time-bound. This structure will help ensure that your goals are clear and attainable.

Smart goal description

1.

2.

3.

- Write down specific actions that you can take to achieve each goal. Think about resources that you might need or strategies that you can implement.

My action steps

1.

2.

3.

- Set up a way to monitor your progress. This could include regular check-ins with yourself or journaling about your experiences.

Review date	Progress summary

- Review your progress after a designated period, for instance, a month. Reflect on what worked, what did not, and how you can adjust your goals or strategies.

What worked well?

What can be improved?

Next steps.

As you work on this worksheet template, remember that life changes, so be open to adjusting your goals as you need to. Acknowledge your progress, no matter how small. It is important to recognize your efforts. Remember that if you find it challenging to achieve your goals, you can always reach out to friends, mentors, or professionals who can support you.

Reflection Questions: Reflecting on Your Goals

Long-term goals can take years to achieve, but they represent your ultimate vision for your life. Consider different areas of your life, including your career, relationships, health, and personal growth. What do you want to accomplish in each area? Write down these goals, and allow yourself to dream big.

Once you've identified your long-term goals, reflect on how they connect to your "why." Ask yourself why these goals matter to you. Do they align with your core values and passions? Understanding this alignment ensures your goals are aspirational and deeply meaningful, which makes them easier to stay committed to.

Finally, consider small, actionable steps you can take today to move closer to your long-term goals. What can you do right now to start building momentum? Remember that, small actions, when taken consistently, can lead to significant progress over time. Write down specific actions you can take, and commit to starting them today.

By regularly reflecting on these questions, you can keep your goals in focus, ensure they remain aligned with your motivations, and maintain the momentum needed to achieve them. This reflective practice clarifies your path forward and reinforces your commitment to achieving success in your life.

Final Thoughts on Motivation and Goal Setting

As you grow and evolve, so will your motivations and goals. Motivation and goal setting are not one-time events; they are lifelong processes. Your motivations will evolve as you experience new things, learn more about yourself, and adapt to changing circumstances. Similarly, your goals will shift as you achieve milestones and set new aspirations.

Embrace this journey as a continuous reflection, action, and growth cycle. Remember, the journey of motivation and goal setting is unique to you. Celebrate your progress, learn from setbacks, and keep moving forward with confidence and determination. Your goals are within reach, and with a clear sense of purpose and a well-structured plan, you have the power to achieve them.

Chapter 7:

Empathy: The Heart of Emotional Intelligence

Empathy is seeing with the eyes of another, listening with the ears of another, and feeling with the heart of another. –Alfred Adler

As Claire worked on her emotional intelligence, she realized that she needed to develop empathy to connect with others. She wanted to do more than understand her own feelings; she wanted to be able to relate to the emotions of the people around her, especially during tough times. It wasn't enough to "feel bad" for someone; Claire wanted to see things from their perspective, even when their experiences differed from hers.

She started by practicing really listening to people, not just hearing what they were saying but paying attention to how they said it and what they were feeling. When friends or family talked to her about their problems, she tried not to jump in with advice or solutions right away. Instead, she would listen and offer simple responses like, "I'm here for you," or "That sounds really hard." This allowed the other person to open up more, and it showed Claire that, sometimes, just being there was the best thing she could do.

Claire also tried to understand emotions she didn't immediately relate to. She wouldn't dismiss their feelings if someone were upset about something that seemed minor to her. Instead, she would try to imagine what it would be like to walk in their shoes, asking herself, "What might this situation feel like if I had the same experiences they did?" This approach helped her respond with understanding rather than judgment. It made a difference, especially in her friendships, where she started noticing deeper and more meaningful conversations.

However, Claire found that connecting with others' emotions came with a risk—sometimes, she would get overwhelmed by the intensity of other people's struggles. There were moments when she felt weighed down by the emotions of others, almost as if they were her own. To keep from burning out, she worked on setting boundaries. She reminded herself that while she could offer support, it wasn't her job to fix everything for everyone. This helped her stay grounded while still caring deeply.

As she continued practicing empathy, Claire noticed positive changes around her. People seemed to trust her more, often turning to her for support because they knew she would listen without judging. She also found herself being more understanding toward her own struggles. When she was going through something difficult, she would think, "If a friend felt this way, how would I respond to them?" The shift in perspective allowed her to treat herself with the same kindness she extended to others. Empathy became central to Claire's emotional development, enabling her to connect with others on a deeper level and approach life with more compassion. It wasn't about being perfect; it was about choosing to see others—and herself—with a more open heart.

Understanding Empathy

At the very heart of emotional intelligence is empathy. It is important because it helps you to be able to connect with others on a deeper level and build trust and understanding. It fosters better communication, reduces conflict, and promotes greater kindness. When you can understand and empathize with how others feel, you can support them, strengthening relationships and creating more compassionate communities.

Some people think empathy and sympathy are the same, but this is not the case. Empathy is about shared emotional experience, while sympathy is about offering condolences or understanding from a more detached perspective.

Empathy is about genuine understanding and sharing someone else's feelings or perspectives; it is almost like putting yourself in their shoes. It is all about recognizing emotions in others and being capable of responding with care and true compassion.

Empathy involves sharing or deeply understanding another person's emotional experience. It is a mutual connection where you experience or intellectually understand what someone else is going through. In contrast, sympathy involves pity or sorrow for someone else's situation without necessarily sharing or understanding their feelings. It's more about acknowledging another person's hardship rather than a shared emotional experience.

Empathy helps build stronger bonds by creating a sense of shared experience and mutual understanding. When people feel understood and validated, they are more likely to open up and build trust.

Sympathy, while well-intentioned, can sometimes create a sense of distance. Feeling pitied rather than understood can lead to feelings of isolation or inferiority, as sympathy may inadvertently highlight a power imbalance.

It is generally accepted that there are three main types of empathy, which include:

- **Cognitive empathy**, which involves understanding someone else's thoughts, emotions, and viewpoints. It is the ability to intellectually grasp what another person is experiencing, even if you don't share the same feelings. It is particularly useful in problem-solving, conflict resolution, and communication.

- **Emotional empathy**, which is the capacity to feel what another person is going through physically. It is an automatic response where you experience a reflection of another person's emotions within yourself, like feeling sadness when someone else is sad. It is important in building deep emotional connections and providing emotional support.

- **Compassionate empathy** goes beyond understanding and feeling; it involves taking proactive steps to help others based on your empathy. It combines the emotional connection of emotional empathy with the cognitive understanding of cognitive empathy, driving compassionate action. It motivates us to give tangible support and advice to those in need.

Empathy develops gradually as you grow up. It starts in early childhood and evolves throughout life. It grows through life experiences, social interactions, and seeing empathy modeled by others.

Age	What happens
Infancy (0-2 years)	Babies begin by reacting to the emotions they see around them, like crying when they hear another baby cry. This is more of an instinctive response to emotions, yet not true empathy.
Early childhood (2-5 years)	Around age 2, children start to understand that other people have feelings. For example, they might comfort an upset friend by offering a toy or a hug. This is the beginning of basic empathy, where they realize, "You are sad, and I want to help."
Late childhood (5-10 years)	As children grow, they develop more cognitive empathy. They start to see things from another person's perspective and recognize that feelings can be complex.

Adolescence and adulthood	Empathy becomes more refined, combining emotional and cognitive aspects. Teens and adults become better at putting themselves in someone else's shoes and understanding their emotions and their point of view.

Empathy involves several brain areas that work together to help you understand and connect with others' emotions. When all these brain regions work together, you can not only recognize what others are feeling (cognitive empathy) but also share in their emotions (emotional empathy). This combination allows you to act with compassionate empathy.

Let's look at how it works:

- **Mirror neurons**: These are special brain cells that fire when you see someone else do something or feel an emotion. For example, if you see someone smile or cry, mirror neurons activate, helping you "mirror" their feelings, which is key for emotional empathy.

- **Anterior insula**: This region is involved in processing your own emotions and recognizing them in others. It helps you feel what someone else might be feeling, like pain or joy.

- **Anterior Cingulate Cortex (ACC)**: This part of the brain helps you regulate emotional responses and is involved in experiencing emotional empathy, like feeling sadness when someone else is sad.

- **Prefrontal cortex**: This is where cognitive empathy happens. The prefrontal cortex helps you understand someone else's perspective and think about why they might feel a certain way.

It allows you to mentally step into their shoes without feeling their emotions.

- **Amygdala**: The amygdala processes emotional reactions, like fear or distress. It alerts you when someone is in distress, helping you to respond with empathy or concern.

The Impact of Empathy on Relationships

When you are able to empathize with others, you show them that their feelings and experiences are valid and understood. This validation fosters trust, as people feel safe to be vulnerable when they know their emotions will be respected and handled with care.

Empathy allows partners to connect on a deeper emotional level. By sharing and understanding each other's emotional experiences, couples can strengthen their bond and create a solid foundation of mutual respect and love.

Additionally, empathy plays a crucial role in conflict resolution by helping you see the situation from the other person's point of view. This understanding can reduce tension, allowing each party to appreciate the emotions and motivations behind the other's actions. By fostering mutual understanding, empathy helps find common ground during disputes, making it easier for both parties to negotiate and resolve conflicts.

Empathy enables you to provide authentic emotional support by connecting with the other person's feelings. This connection makes your support more meaningful, as it comes from a shared experience and understanding.

Providing empathetic support during difficult times can significantly strengthen relationships. It reassures others that they are not alone in their struggles, which can be incredibly comforting and empowering.

Empathy in Professional Relationships

Empathy helps team members understand and appreciate each other's strengths, weaknesses, and working styles. This understanding fosters a collaborative environment where everyone feels valued and respected.

Conflict arises even in the workplace, but empathy allows conflict resolution by promoting understanding and open communication. When team members feel heard and understood, they are likelier to work harmoniously.

Leaders who demonstrate empathy can better understand their team members' needs, concerns, and motivations. This understanding enables them to make decisions in the best interest of their employees and the organization.

Empathetic leaders foster a positive, inclusive work culture where employees feel supported and valued. This culture can lead to increased job satisfaction, loyalty, and productivity.

When it comes to customer service, empathy allows professionals to understand and address clients' needs and concerns genuinely. This understanding leads to better service and stronger client relationships. If customers feel that their concerns are understood and taken seriously, they are likelier to remain loyal to a company. Empathy helps in building trust and long-term relationships with clients.

Empathy in Society

Empathy is a great tool for promoting social harmony. By bridging social, cultural, and ideological divides, empathy promotes understanding and accepting diverse perspectives. When people empathize with each other, it leads to greater social cohesion and harmony.

Empathy encourages tolerance and respect for differences in reducing social tensions and conflicts. It helps people appreciate the common humanity that connects us despite our differences.

True empathy allows us to see beyond stereotypes and biases by encouraging us to understand people as unique human beings rather than as members of a particular group. This understanding can help reduce prejudice and discrimination.

By fostering a deeper understanding of the experiences of marginalized groups, empathy can drive social change and promote equality. It motivates people to stand against injustice and advocate for those who are disadvantaged.

Empathy is the cornerstone of community building. It fosters strong, supportive networks where people look out for each other and work together for the common good. Communities built on empathy are more resilient and better equipped to tackle challenges. Empathy-driven community action can lead to positive social change and improved quality of life for all members.

Empathy in Difficult Situations

Showing empathy can be challenging in certain situations, possibly due to emotional, social, or contextual barriers. Some examples of these situations include when:

- Someone's experience is foreign to you.

- You disagree with someone else's feelings or perspectives.

- You are emotionally overwhelmed yourself.

- The person is seeking empathy for a mistake.

- You feel a person is overreacting.

- A situation is repetitive.

- You feel judged or attacked.

In situations like these, finding empathy often involves recognizing the other person's humanity and emotions, even when it is uncomfortable or their feelings differ from yours. Here are some strategies that you can use to maintain empathy:

- **Stay grounded:** In challenging interactions, staying grounded and not letting the other person's behavior trigger a negative response are important. Focus on your emotions and remain calm, which will help you maintain empathy even in tough situations.

- **Be patient:** Difficult people or situations often require extra patience. Everyone has struggles, and their behavior might reflect their pain or challenges.

- **Use empathy for de-escalation:** Empathy can be a powerful tool for defusing difficult situations. Acknowledging the other person's feelings and showing understanding can reduce tension and create a more constructive dialogue.

It's possible to empathize with someone without necessarily agreeing with their actions or beliefs. This approach allows you to maintain empathy even when you strongly disagree with the other person.

While empathy involves understanding and sharing another's feelings, holding people accountable for their actions is also important. Maintaining this balance can be challenging, but is crucial for healthy relationships.

Enhancing Empathetic Skills

Self-awareness involves understanding your emotions, thoughts, and behaviors. This self-understanding is crucial for empathy because it allows you to recognize and regulate your emotions, making it easier to understand and connect with others' feelings.

EI begins with self-awareness. By being in tune with your emotions, you can better understand how they influence your interactions with others, which is a key component of developing empathy.

To enhance your self-awareness and develop empathy, you can consider the following:

- Mindfulness meditation can help you become more aware of your emotions and how they affect your thoughts and behaviors.

- Regularly journaling about your feelings and experiences can help you reflect on your emotional responses and understand them better.

- Setting aside time daily to check in with your emotions. Identify your feelings and why, and consider how these emotions might impact your interactions with others.

- Practice empathy by performing small acts of kindness for others. These acts can brighten someone's day and demonstrate that you care about their well-being.

- Regularly reflect on your interactions to assess how well you've practiced empathy. Identify areas for improvement and set goals to enhance your empathetic skills over time.

Another way that you can develop your empathy is through active listening. Active listening involves fully concentrating, understanding, and responding to what others are saying. It's a fundamental aspect of empathy because it shows that you value the speaker's perspective and are genuinely interested in their experience.

When people feel heard, they are more likely to open up, creating a stronger connection. Active listening helps build trust and rapport, which is essential for empathetic relationships. Techniques for active listening include:

- Maintaining eye contact: Eye contact shows that you are focused and engaged in the conversation, making the speaker feel valued and understood.

- Avoiding interruptions: Allow the speaker to express themselves fully without interrupting. This demonstrates respect and patience.

- Paraphrasing: After the speaker has finished, paraphrase what they've said to confirm your understanding. This technique shows that you are actively processing their words and helps clarify any misunderstandings.

Understanding Others, Overcoming Biases, Nonverbal Communication, and Expressing Empathy

- Practice imagining how you would feel in another person's situation. Consider their background, experiences, and emotions to understand their perspective better.

- Engage in open-ended questioning to gain deeper insights into the other person's thoughts and feelings. This approach encourages them to share more and helps you see things from their point of view.

- In order to overcome biases, you first need to identify them. Reflect on your beliefs and biases that may affect your ability to empathize with certain people or groups. Acknowledge these biases to prevent them from influencing your interactions. Actively challenge stereotypes and assumptions you hold about others. Try to learn more about people different from you to broaden your understanding and reduce biases.

- It is important that you are able to interpret nonverbal signals. Pay attention to body language, facial expressions, and tone of voice to gain insights into how someone feels. Nonverbal cues often reveal emotions that are not expressed verbally.

- Notice when someone's nonverbal cues don't match their words, which might indicate hidden emotions or discomfort. Address these discrepancies with sensitivity to better understand their true feelings.

- Use open and relaxed body language to show you are approachable and engaged. Nodding, leaning slightly forward, and maintaining appropriate eye contact can signal empathy.

- Mirror the other person's emotions with your facial expressions to convey understanding and empathy. For example, a soft smile or a concerned expression can show that you are in tune with their feelings.

Overcoming "Empathy" Challenges

Constantly empathizing with others, especially in emotionally intense situations, can lead to emotional fatigue, also known as "compassion fatigue." This occurs when the emotional weight of understanding and sharing others' feelings becomes overwhelming, leading to burnout.

Understanding the symptoms of emotional exhaustion, like feeling drained, detached, or experiencing a lack of motivation, can help you identify when empathy is becoming too taxing.

You can manage emotional fatigue by:
- Engaging in regular self-care activities to replenish your emotional energy. This could include physical activities, hobbies, meditation, or spending time in nature.

- Seeking support when you feel overwhelmed. Talking to a friend, mentor, or therapist can relieve and help you process your emotions.

- Using mindfulness and relaxation techniques can help you stay grounded and prevent empathy from becoming overwhelming. Techniques like deep breathing, meditation, or progressive muscle relaxation can be particularly effective.

Boundaries and Empathy

While empathy is crucial for connecting with others, setting boundaries is essential to protect your emotional well-being. Healthy boundaries ensure you can be empathetic without taking on others' emotions as your own.

Recognize your emotional boundaries and know when you need to step back to recharge. Setting clear boundaries can prevent you from becoming overly involved in others' issues to the detriment of your mental health.

Here are some strategies for setting and maintaining healthy boundaries:

- **Communicate your boundaries:** Be open and honest about your limits with others. This may involve politely declining to engage in certain discussions or taking time for yourself when needed.

- **Be assertive:** Assertiveness is key to maintaining boundaries while still being empathetic. It's about standing up for your own needs while respecting the needs of others.

- **Reflect:** Periodically reflect on your boundaries to ensure they remain effective and appropriate. Adjust them as necessary based on your emotional state and the demands of your relationships.

Reflection Questions

When was the last time you felt true empathy for someone else? What did that experience teach you about your empathetic abilities?

What biases might be affecting your ability to empathize with others? How can you overcome these biases?

Do you have clear boundaries to protect your emotional well-being while being empathetic? How can you improve these boundaries?

Empathy Challenges

Please use the space below each challenge to write about your experience.

Perspective Day

Spend a day consciously trying to see situations from others' perspectives, whether in your relationships, at work, or even during everyday interactions like shopping or commuting.

Listening Challenge

Choose a day focused solely on listening during conversations. Make a point not to offer advice or opinions, but rather listen and acknowledge the other person's feelings.

Compassionate Action

Identify a situation where someone needs help, and take action, whether it's offering emotional support, practical assistance, or simply being there for them. Reflect on how this made you feel and impacted the other person.

Recommended Books and Articles on Empathy

Books

- *The Empathy Effect* by Helen Riess, MD: A comprehensive exploration of empathy from a neuroscientific perspective, offering practical strategies for enhancing empathy in everyday life and professional settings.

- *Empathy: Why It Matters, and How to Get It* by **Roman Krznaric**: This book delves into the importance of empathy in human interactions and provides actionable insights on cultivating empathy in both personal and social contexts.

- *The War for Kindness: Building Empathy in a Fractured World* by **Jamil Zaki**: Zaki's book argues that empathy is not a fixed trait, but a skill that can be developed. He offers inspiring stories and scientific evidence to show how empathy can be nurtured to create a more compassionate world.

Articles

- **"The Science of Empathy"**: An in-depth article examines empathy's scientific underpinnings, including how it develops, its benefits, and ways to foster it. This piece is a great resource for understanding the biological and psychological mechanisms behind empathy.

- **"Why Empathy Is Essential"**: This article explores the current state of empathy in society, discussing the factors that threaten its presence and its vital role in maintaining human connections.

- **"Empathy in Leadership: How to Lead With Compassion"**: Focused on the professional sphere, this article provides insights into how leaders can incorporate empathy into their leadership style to foster a positive and productive workplace.

Chapter 8:

Reading Social Cues

Humans are social beings, and we are happier, and better, when connected to others.
—Paul Bloom

As Claire continued her self-empowerment journey with emotional intelligence, she realized that understanding social cues was an essential piece of the puzzle. While she had made strides in practicing empathy and emotional awareness, she struggled to read the subtle signals people gave off in various situations. However, with each small step she took, she felt a sense of accomplishment, knowing that recognizing these cues could enhance her connections and help her respond better in conversations.

To improve her skills, Claire started observing people in everyday situations, such as at the coffee shop, family gatherings, and even on public transport. By observing facial expressions, body language, and tone of voice, she realized how much could be conveyed without words. For instance, she learned to recognize when someone felt uncomfortable, even if they smiled politely. A slight furrow of the brow or crossed arms often signaled that someone might need a bit of space or understanding.

Claire also began to pay attention to her own body language. She realized that her posture, gestures, and facial expressions communicated her feelings even when she wasn't speaking. By aligning her body language with her emotions, she found she could create a more authentic connection with others. During a difficult conversation, she learned to lean in and maintain eye contact, which showed support and encouraged her friend to open up.

Claire decided to read books and articles on nonverbal communication to enhance her understanding of social cues further. She learned that different cultures could interpret cues uniquely, adding another layer to her awareness. This knowledge helped her navigate diverse social settings, ensuring she approached interactions sensitively and respectfully.

Claire also practiced asking open-ended questions during conversations. Instead of jumping straight into advice or solutions, she would say things like, "How did that make you feel?" or "What do you think you'll do next?" These questions encouraged others to share more about their experiences, allowing Claire to gauge their emotional state better and respond appropriately. The more she practiced this, the more comfortable she became in reading the room and adapting her approach based on the vibe she picked up.

Over time, Claire noticed a significant shift in her relationships. Being more attuned to social cues made her feel more connected to those around her. She felt a deeper sense of empathy and understanding, and this was reciprocated by her friends and family. They started to express gratitude for her understanding nature, and she found that conflicts decreased. Instead of misunderstanding each other, they could communicate more openly, allowing for a deeper level of trust and connection.

As Claire learned about social cues, she realized it was not just about improving her interactions, but also about becoming more self-aware. Understanding how she came across to others helped her strengthen her emotional responses and become a better communicator. Each step she took led to increased emotional intelligence, better relationships, and a stronger sense of belonging. She felt more included and part of a community, and this sense of belonging was a powerful motivator in her journey.

Understanding Social Cues

Being able to understand social cues, especially non-verbal communication, is fundamental to building strong, meaningful relationships. Much of what people express isn't spoken in words but through subtle signals that show someone's true feelings, emotions, and thoughts. By paying attention to verbal and non-verbal elements, you are able to gain a fuller picture of what someone is communicating and can react with greater sensitivity and awareness.

Verbal communication—what is spoken—provides explicit information, but non-verbal cues often reveal the deeper, unspoken emotions behind the words. For instance, someone might say they are "fine," but their crossed arms or strained voice may suggest otherwise.

Understanding and being aware of social cues bring numerous benefits, especially when it comes to emotional intelligence (EI) and building effective relationships. Some key advantages include

- improved communication
- stronger relationships
- enhanced empathy
- conflict resolution
- increased persuasion and influence
- improved adaptability
- boosted EI
- better teamwork and collaboration
- increased social comfort and confidence
- enhanced leadership skills

Some examples of important social cues that can help you in your everyday interactions and relationships include:

Social cue	Example
Facial expressions	Smiling: can indicate friendliness, happiness, or approval.
	Frowning: can show confusion, disagreement, or frustration.
	Raised eyebrows: often signals surprise, curiosity, or disbelief.
Eyes contact	Direct eye contact: often shows interest, confidence, or engagement.
	Avoiding eye contact: might signal discomfort, shyness, or dishonesty.
	Frequent glancing: can suggest nervousness or distraction.
Body language	Open posture: signals receptiveness and comfort.
	Crossed arms: may indicate defensiveness and discomfort.
	Leaning in: shows interest and attentiveness.
	Leaning back: can suggest disinterest, relaxation, or withdrawal.

Tone of voice	Calm and steady tone: indicates control and confidence.
	High-pitched or loud voice: might suggest excitement, anger, or nervousness.
	Monotone: could signal boredom, disinterest, or emotional distance.
Gestures	Nodding: often used to show agreement or understanding.
	Pointing: used for directing attention but can be seen as aggressive in some contexts.
	Hand movements: can emphasize speech or express excitement.
Personal space	Standing close: might indicate comfort or intimacy.
	Stepping back: could signal a need for distance or discomfort.
Silence	Pausing: can signal thoughtfulness or give space for the other person to speak.
	Long silences: might indicate awkwardness, anger, or discomfort.

Touch

Patting on the back: often a gesture of support or encouragement.

Handshake: a common form of greeting, with firmness signaling confidence.

Hugging: can show affection or comfort, but may not be appropriate in all situations.

Active vs Passive Listening

In today's world, with so many distractions like phones and social media, active listening has become even more important for meaningful connections and clear communication. Active listening means that you are fully focused on the person who is talking to you. You are not just hearing the words that are coming out of their mouths, but you are really understanding what they mean. You might ask questions, nod, or even summarize what they have said to make sure that you are on the same page.

A good example of active listening would be if a friend was sharing a problem that they are having with you. You might say. "So, you are feeling upset because you think that your boss is not truly valuing your work? Did I get that right?"

Then, you get passive listening. Passive listening is when you hear what the person has to say but are not fully engaged or focused. It is more like a background noise. You are not making a real effort to understand, ask questions, or give any feedback.

An example of passive listening would be if the same friend were sharing a personal problem with you, and you only nod occasionally and do not respond much. If you respond in this way, you are likely a passive listener.

With that said, both active and passive listening have their place and benefits. Being able to develop a healthy balance between the two can be useful in different contexts. Let's have a quick look at the benefits of each of these:

Benefits of active listening	Benefits of passive listening
• improved understanding	• efficient multitasking
• build trust and rapport	• exposure to new ideas
• encourages openness	• less mentally taxing
• enhances problem-solving	• time-efficient
• boosts EI	• reduced conflict
• increased retention	

Active listening can be beneficial in the following contexts:

Context	Example
Conflict resolution	When trying to solve disputes or disagreements, active listening helps ensure all parties feel heard and understood.
Workplace collaboration	During team meetings or brainstorming sessions, active listening improves communication and strengthens teamwork.

Counseling or support roles	In therapeutic or coaching environments, being an active listener shows empathy and helps people open up about personal challenges.
Learning environments	In classrooms, training, or workshops, active listening helps in grasping complex concepts and asking clarifying questions.
Negotiations	Whether in business or personal settings, actively listening to the other side's needs and concerns can help in finding mutually beneficial solutions
Building relationships	In personal or professional settings, active listening strengthens emotional bonds and fosters trust.
Parenting	When children express feelings or concerns, active listening validates their emotions and supports their emotional development.
Public speaking engagements	If you're part of an audience with Q&A sessions, actively listening will help you ask insightful questions and make meaningful contributions.

Passive listening can be beneficial in the following contexts:

Context	Example
While multitasking	When performing routine tasks (e.g., cleaning, commuting), passive listening to podcasts, audiobooks, or news helps you absorb information without full focus.
Background learning	While consuming media like documentaries, news, or radio shows, you can gather useful insights without engaging deeply.
Casual conversations	In light social settings where active engagement isn't required, passive listening allows you to remain polite while staying slightly detached.
Crowded or noisy environments	When it's hard to hear clearly, like in public spaces, passive listening can help you pick up bits of information even if active engagement isn't possible.
When decompressing	Sometimes, after a long day, passive listening to soothing music, light TV shows, or relaxing podcasts allows for mental rest without much focus.
Long lectures or presentations	If the material is repetitive or less relevant to you, passive listening allows you to remain present without expending mental energy.

Low-stake meetings	In meetings where your direct input isn't needed, passive listening can help you stay informed while focusing on other tasks.
When someone needs to vent	Sometimes, people need to talk without requiring advice or deep engagement. Passive listening lets them get things off their chest while you lend an ear.

Distinguishing Between Active and Passive Listening

Recognizing whether someone is actively or passively listening to you can help you gauge how engaged someone is in a conversation. Here are some signs that can help you to distinguish between active and passive listening:

Signs of active listening	**Signs of passive listening**
Eye contact: The person maintains eye contact, showing they're engaged.	Lack of eye contact: They may look away frequently or seem distracted.
Nodding: They nod occasionally to signal understanding and encouragement.	Minimal response: They offer few verbal affirmations or responses.
Verbal affirmations: They use phrases like "I see," "I understand," or "That makes sense."	Distractions: They may be preoccupied with their phone, computer, or other distractions.
Asking questions: They ask follow-up questions to clarify or deepen the conversation.	Short answers: Their responses may be brief and not invite further discussion.

Summarizing: They paraphrase or summarize what you've said to confirm understanding.	Failure to follow up: They don't ask questions or refer back to things you've said later.
Body language: They face you, lean slightly forward, and exhibit open body language.	Closed body language: They may cross their arms or turn away, indicating disinterest.
Emotional responses: They respond appropriately to your emotions (e.g., showing empathy or concern).	

Reading the Room: Navigating Social Situations

The more you interact with others, the better you'll become at reading and responding to social cues. Before engaging in a conversation, it's essential to gauge the emotional tone of the room to avoid missteps and ensure a positive interaction.

Reading the rooms means paying close attention to the atmosphere and the energy of the group, as it can heavily influence how your message will be received. For example, entering a lively, upbeat room may require a more enthusiastic approach, while a quieter, somber environment might call for a softer, more considerate tone.

To read the room effectively, observe the non-verbal cues of those present. Ask yourself if people are

- smiling
- laughing
- leaning in toward one another

Or do they seem closed off, with:

- crossed arms

- minimal eye contact

- tense facial expressions

These cues provide insights into the group's dynamics and emotions, allowing you to adapt your behavior and engage more appropriately. By assessing the mood before diving into a conversation, you set the stage for smoother communication and a better understanding of others' needs and expectations.

Another effective way to adapt your behavior based on social cues is by adjusting your tone of voice. Non-verbal cues from your listener, like their body language, facial expressions, or level of engagement, can give important feedback on how they're receiving your message.

If someone seems distracted, offering minimal eye contact or fidgeting, you might need to adjust by lowering your voice or slowing down your speech to recapture their attention. On the other hand, if they appear engaged, with focused eye contact and open body language, maintaining an energetic and enthusiastic tone can help keep the conversation flowing.

Adaptation is key. For example, if you're in a formal setting and your listener appears tense, using a calm and measured tone can help ease the situation. However, in a casual or light-hearted setting, a more relaxed, humorous tone may be more appropriate. Recognizing and adjusting based on these non-verbal cues helps to maintain harmony and ensures that the listener feels comfortable and understood.

Mirroring is a rather subtle technique that involves matching the body language, tone, and energy level of the person you're speaking with. This doesn't mean copying their every move but rather reflecting their general posture, pace, and expressions to create rapport and trust. For example, if someone is speaking slowly and calmly, mirroring their pace and demeanor can help you appear more aligned with them. On the other hand, if they're enthusiastic and animated, responding with similar energy helps you build a connection.

Mirroring helps people feel understood on a deeper, subconscious level. It creates a sense of comfort and makes interactions feel more natural, leading to stronger connections and smoother communication.

It is important to remember that awkward moments in social situations are inevitable, but how you handle them can make all the difference. The key to recovering from an awkward interaction is to read social cues and adjust your behavior accordingly.

If you say something that seems to fall flat, watch for signs of discomfort—like forced smiles, shifting body language, or avoiding eye contact. Instead of pushing the conversation further in that direction, pivot gracefully by changing the topic or lightening the mood with a friendly, self-deprecating comment like, "Well, that didn't land as I hoped!"

Recognizing signs of discomfort in others is equally important. If someone seems uneasy, like crossing their arms or looking away frequently, try to steer the conversation toward something more neutral or ask open-ended questions that allow them to share their thoughts at their own pace. By acknowledging awkwardness and using social cues to course-correct, you can turn uncomfortable moments into opportunities to create more relaxed, positive interactions.

Interactive Element; Listening Skills Exercise

By reflecting on the questions below, you'll gain insight into how well you can distinguish between active and passive listening and improve your overall communication skills.

Consider a recent interaction; how did passive listening affect your ability to understand the speaker's message?

When you shifted to active listening, how did the conversation change? Did you notice a difference in the speaker's tone, body language, or engagement?

How well were you able to tune into both what was said (verbal) and how it was communicated (non-verbal)?

What aspects of active listening felt natural, and what felt challenging?

Reflection and Self-Assessment: How Well Do You Read Non-Verbal Cues?

How often do you notice people's body language in conversation? Do you pay attention to whether someone is leaning in, crossing their arms, or using other gestures that can indicate their emotions?

Do I frequently misinterpret tone of voice? Have you ever mistaken excitement for anger or confusion for disinterest due to a misunderstanding of tone?

How do I know if someone is truly listening to me? Can you pick up on whether someone is genuinely engaged based on their eye contact, nodding, or facial expressions?

Final Thought on This Chapter

Improving your ability to read social cues takes practice and awareness. Remember to stay present in the moment, and focus on the person speaking. Next time you interact with others, consider how well you read social cues and whether you missed any non-verbal signals.

Chapter 9:

Cultural and Generational Awareness

> *The greatest discovery of my generation is that a human being can alter his life by altering his attitudes.* –William James

Claire's journey to greater emotional intelligence was strengthened with each step she took. *Emotional Intelligence: Your Ultimate Hands-On Guide* helped her realize the importance of cultural and generational awareness.

While Claire's understanding of her emotions and social cues improved, she realized these skills alone were not enough. She needed to recognize the unique backgrounds and experiences of others, as different cultures and generations often express emotions and communicate in distinct ways. Determined to learn more about these differences, Claire set out on a journey to greater understanding.

To broaden her understanding, Claire spoke with friends and family from various backgrounds. She asked about their traditions and values to see how their cultures shaped their emotions. Claire learned that while emotions are universal, expressions can differ. Some cultures express emotions openly, while others value restraint. This insight helped Claire engage in conversations with more sensitivity and respect.

With the help of literature and documentaries about different cultures, Claire learned how community and family values influence emotional expression. This awareness helped her understand that when friends from other cultures struggled to share personal feelings, it reflected a different approach to relationships rather than a lack of emotion.

When it came to generational differences, Claire realized that her experiences as a millennial were different from those of her parents and grandparents, who had grown up in very different social and economic environments. She spoke to her family members to learn more and asked them about their childhood experiences and how societal expectations shaped their emotional lives. These discussions taught Claire to adapt her communication style based on others' cultural and generational backgrounds.

Claire's emotional intelligence grew as she learned about different cultures and generations. Embracing diverse experiences helped her build deeper relationships and connect better with others, enriching her life and those around her.

Connecting Emotional Intelligence, Cultural, and Generational Awareness

Emotional intelligence is key for interacting with people from different cultures and ages. It helps you recognize and manage feelings, which improves communication and empathy. Being aware of your emotions and the emotions of others is important for building real relationships and connecting across cultures and generations.

Here are some ways that EI can benefit you in diverse interactions, like when dealing with cultural and generational differences:

- **Better communication:** EI helps you understand your own feelings and the emotions of others, leading to clearer and more effective conversations.
- **Increased empathy:** You'll be more able to put yourself in someone else's shoes, helping you to appreciate their perspective and experiences, especially if they come from a different culture or generation.

- **Improved relationships:** By recognizing and respecting emotional cues, you can build stronger, more trusting relationships with people from various backgrounds.

- **Conflict resolution:** EI gives you the skills to navigate disagreements calmly and constructively, making it easier to find common ground.

- **Adaptability:** You'll be more flexible in your approach to different people, allowing you to adjust your communication style to fit the needs of various cultural or generational contexts.

- **Enhanced collaboration:** Working with diverse teams becomes easier because you can understand different viewpoints and work styles, leading to more effective teamwork.

- **Cultural sensitivity:** With emotional intelligence, you learn to appreciate and respect cultural differences, helping you avoid misunderstandings and promote inclusivity.

- **Open-mindedness:** This skill encourages you to be open to new ideas and perspectives, making you more receptive to learning from others, regardless of their background.

By developing your emotional intelligence, you can navigate diverse interactions more smoothly and create meaningful connections with people from all walks of life. Here are some ways you can develop your emotional intelligence, cultural awareness, and generational awareness:

- **Practice active listening:** Focus on really hearing what others are saying without interrupting. Show genuine interest in their thoughts and feelings. This helps you understand their perspectives better.

- **Engage in cultural activities:** Attend cultural events, workshops, or festivals in your community. This exposure helps you appreciate different traditions, values, and ways of life.

- **Read diverse books and articles:** Choose literature or articles that represent different cultures and generations. This can provide insights into their experiences and perspectives, helping you understand and relate to them better.

- **Have open conversations:** Talk to people from different backgrounds and age groups. Ask questions about their experiences and opinions, and be open to learning from them.

- **Reflect on your emotions:** Take time each day to check in with yourself about your feelings. Journaling about your emotions and reactions can help you understand patterns and improve your emotional awareness.

- **Seek feedback:** Ask family or friends for feedback on your emotional responses and interactions. This can help you see areas where you can improve your emotional intelligence.

- **Learn about different communication styles:** Research how different cultures and generations prefer to communicate. This can help you adjust your approach and connect more effectively.

- **Participate in empathy exercises:** Practice putting yourself in someone else's shoes by imagining their feelings and reactions in various situations. This strengthens your ability to empathize with others.

- **Join workshops or training:** Look for workshops or courses on emotional intelligence, cultural competency, or generational differences. These can provide structured learning and practical skills.

- **Stay curious and open-minded:** Approach new experiences and conversations with a mindset of curiosity. Being open to learning allows you to grow in your understanding of others.

By incorporating these practices into your daily life, you'll enhance your EI and become more aware of the cultural and generational differences around you.

Cultural Awareness

Understanding emotions is important for building strong relationships in today's connected world. Emotional intelligence is a crucial skill that can improve how you interact with people from different cultures. By developing your EI, you can recognize, understand, and manage your own emotions and those of others, which helps you communicate better with people from diverse backgrounds.

Culture is multidimensional, influencing various aspects of life, including:

- **Language**: The primary medium through which cultural knowledge is transmitted. Language reflects the values and priorities of a culture, shaping how people think and communicate.

- **Traditions**: Rituals, customs, and practices passed down through generations. These traditions help to maintain cultural identity and continuity.

- **Values**: Core principles and beliefs that guide behavior and decision-making. Values differ significantly across cultures, influencing what is considered right or wrong, important or trivial.

- **Worldview**: Culture determines how people perceive reality, including their beliefs about time, space, and the nature of existence. For example, some cultures prioritize collective well-being over individual achievements, while others emphasize personal autonomy and success.

- **Behavior**: Cultural norms and values dictate appropriate behavior in various contexts. For instance, cultures with high regard for elders may encourage young people to show deference and respect to older people.

- **Identity**: Culture is a key component of identity, providing people with a sense of belonging and continuity. It influences everything from personal values and ethics to social roles and expectations.

Below are some other important cultural differences to consider regarding emotional intelligence. Understanding these cultural differences can help facilitate better communication and enhance EI in diverse settings.

- **Expressing feelings:** People from different cultures have distinct ways of showing their feelings. For example, in some cultures, keeping emotions in check is seen as a sign of strength, while in others, openly sharing emotions is encouraged.

- **Ways of communicating:** In cultures that rely on high-context communication, people often use body language and subtle cues to convey their messages. Conversely, in low-context cultures, straightforward and clear language takes precedence.

- **Self vs. community:** Cultures that prioritize individualism celebrate personal achievements and independence. In contrast, collectivist cultures place a higher value on community, relationships, and the well-being of the group.

- **Views on conflict:** How people understand and manage conflict differs across cultures. Some cultures view conflicts as opportunities for growth and discussion, while others might shy away from confrontation, seeing it as undesirable.

- **Respecting authority:** In cultures characterized by high-power distance, showing respect for authority figures and adhering to hierarchies is common, especially in emotional discussions. On the other hand, low-power distance cultures often promote equality in relationships, fostering open dialogue.

- **Openness to vulnerability:** Different cultures have varying attitudes toward vulnerability. In some, displaying vulnerability is seen as a courageous act that fosters connection, while in others, it may be viewed as a weakness, influencing how people communicate their needs for support.

- **Understanding other's feelings:** Cultural differences shape how empathy is understood and expressed. This can affect how people relate to one another and respond to emotional situations, with diverse interpretations across different backgrounds.

- **Privacy norms:** Attitudes toward discussing personal emotions vary widely. In some cultures, sharing feelings openly is perfectly acceptable, while in others, this behavior may be considered inappropriate or overly invasive.

Exercise: Building Emotional Intelligence in Cultural Awareness

This exercise encourages deep reflection, fosters understanding, and builds empathy, ultimately enhancing your emotional intelligence and cultural awareness.

Step 1: Reflect on Your Cultural Background

Take a moment to think about your own cultural identity. Write down your cultural background, traditions, values, and influences that have shaped who you are. Ask yourself questions like:

- What cultural traditions did you grow up with?

- How do these traditions influence your daily life and interactions?

Step 2: Explore Other Cultures

Choose a culture that interests you but is different from your own. Spend some time learning about it. You can read articles, watch documentaries, or listen to interviews. Focus on understanding their values, traditions, and ways of expressing emotions. Write down your findings.

Step 3: Connect Through Conversations

Reach out to someone from that culture (a friend, colleague, or acquaintance) and ask if they'd be willing to share their experiences and perspectives. Approach this conversation with curiosity and openness. Use questions like:

- What are some important traditions in your culture?

- How do people in your culture express emotions?

Step 4: Reflect on the Differences

After your conversations and research, reflect on what you've learned. Think about how this culture's values and emotional expressions differ from your own. Write a few paragraphs about your insights, recognizing both the similarities and differences. Ask yourself:

- How can these insights help you understand others better?

- In what ways might this new perspective change how you interact with people from this culture?

Step 5: Put It Into Practice

Find a way to integrate what you've learned into your daily life. This could be embracing an aspect of their culture, adopting a more open approach in conversations, or simply being more mindful of cultural differences in future interactions. Set a small goal for yourself, like initiating a conversation with someone from a different background or attending a cultural event.

Final reflection: After some time, revisit your reflections and experiences. How have your views changed? How has your EI evolved in the realm of cultural awareness? Write down your thoughts and commit to continuing this journey of learning and growth.

Generational Awareness

Emotional intelligence and generational awareness are closely connected because understanding emotions helps you relate better to people from different age groups. Being emotionally intelligent means being aware of your own feelings and the feelings of others. When you're emotionally aware, you can recognize how different emotions influence people's communication and behavior.

Generational awareness means understanding the experiences, values, and perspectives of different generations, such as Baby Boomers, Gen

X, Millennials, and Gen Z. Each generation has grown up in different times and circumstances, which shapes how they feel and express themselves.

When you combine these two types of awareness, you can better understand why someone from a different generation might react a certain way or communicate differently. This understanding can help you connect with them more effectively, leading to better relationships and teamwork in society.

Below are some important generational differences to consider regarding emotional intelligence. Understanding these generational differences can enhance interpersonal relationships and EI across various age groups.

- **Communication preferences:** Each generation has a unique way of connecting. For example, while some prefer a quick text or video call, others may feel that a coffee chat is more meaningful.

- **Expression of emotions:** Younger people often wear their hearts on their sleeves, sharing feelings openly, whereas older folks might keep emotions tucked away for professionalism, like maintaining a calm demeanor during stressful meetings.

- **Workplace expectations:** Younger workers typically crave jobs that matter to them and want ongoing feedback, like asking for regular check-ins with managers, while older employees might prioritize stability and clear job roles.

- **Attitudes toward authority:** Older generations often respect established hierarchies, expecting to follow the chain of command, while younger people prefer collaborative environments, where everyone's opinion matters, like brainstorming sessions.

- **Conflict resolution styles:** Some generations jump right into discussions to sort out disputes, while others might steer clear of confrontation, preferring to mediate or let conflicts simmer down naturally.

- **Empathy and social issues:** Many young people are passionate about social justice and pushing for empathy in workplace values, such as advocating for mental health days or inclusive practices.

- **Technology and emotional connections:** Those raised in the digital age often use social media to connect emotionally, which can differently shape their interactions compared to older generations, who might value face-to-face conversations more.

- **Coping mechanisms:** Life experiences across generations influence how people deal with stress. For instance, older generations might rely on traditional methods like talking with friends, while younger ones could turn to online communities for support.

Let's look at the experiences, values, and perspectives of different generations in modern society:

Baby Boomers (Born 1946-1964)

- **Experiences:** Grew up during post-war prosperity, civil rights movements, and significant technological changes like the introduction of television.

- **Values:** Hard work, loyalty to employers, and traditional family structures.

- **Perspectives:** Often value face-to-face communication and may prefer stability in their careers.

Generation X (Born 1965-1980)

- **Experiences:** Witnessed the rise of personal computers, the internet, and economic uncertainty, such as the recession in the early 2000s.

- **Values:** Independence, work-life balance, and skepticism of authority.

- **Perspectives:** They often value flexibility in the workplace and may prioritize family time over work commitments.

Millennials (Born 1981-1996)

- **Experiences:** Came of age during the internet boom and the global financial crisis, leading to student debt and job market challenges.

- **Values:** Diversity, social responsibility, and experiences over material goods.

- **Perspectives:** They tend to embrace technology and prefer working in collaborative, inclusive environments.

Generation Z (Born 1997-2012)

- **Experiences:** Grew up with smartphones and social media, facing issues like climate change and social justice movements from a young age.

- **Values:** Authenticity, mental health awareness, and activism for social and environmental causes.

- **Perspectives:** They are often more open to discussing mental health and prefer clear communication through digital platforms. Each generation brings unique experiences, values, and perspectives that shape how they interact with the world.

Exercise: Building Emotional Intelligence in Generational Awareness

This exercise is meant to encourage deep reflection and empathy, allowing you to enhance your emotional intelligence by appreciating the diverse experiences and perspectives of different generations.

Step 1: Reflect On Your Own Generation

Start by thinking about your generation. Write down your birth year and some key events, trends, or experiences that define your generation. Ask yourself questions like:

- What cultural or historical events have shaped my values and beliefs?

- How do I communicate and connect with others from my generation?

Step 2: Learn About Other Generations

Choose two other generations that interest you, for example, Baby Boomers, Generation X, Millennials, or Generation Z. Spend some time researching these generations. Look for articles, videos, or books that explain their experiences, values, and perspectives. Write down what you discover about:

- major life events and social influences

- preferences in communication and work styles

Step 3: Connect with People from Different Generations

Reach out to people from the generations you researched. This can be family members, colleagues, or friends. Spend time chatting and approach the conversation with curiosity. Use questions like:

- What are some experiences that have shaped your life?

- How do you see work and relationships differently compared to my generation?

Step 4: Reflect on the Insights

After your conversations, take some time to reflect on what you learned. Write down the key differences and similarities in values, communication styles, and perspectives. Consider questions like:

- What surprised me about their views?

- How can understanding these differences improve my relationships and teamwork with people from other generations?

Step 5: Practice Empathy and Adaptation

Think about how you can use your insights in daily interactions. Set a goal to adapt your communication style when interacting with different generations. For example, if you're talking to an older colleague, you might focus on being more respectful and patient in conversations. If you're connecting with a younger person, you could try to be more open and casual in your approach.

Final reflection: After a few weeks, revisit your reflections and experiences. Consider how understanding generational differences has impacted your EI and relationships. Write down any changes you've noticed in how you communicate and interact. Commit to continuing this journey of learning and growing in generational awareness.

Further Resources

Below are resources that offer valuable insights and tools for enhancing cultural and generational awareness.

Books

- *The Culture Map* by **Erin Meyer** explores how different cultures interact and communicate in the workplace, offering insights into cross-cultural management and collaboration.

- *Cultural Intelligence: CQ: The Competitive Edge for Leaders Crossing Borders* by **Julia Middleton** provides a guide to developing cultural intelligence and leveraging it for effective leadership and global interactions.

- *Generations: The History of America's Future, 1584 to 2069* by **William Strauss and Neil Howe** offers an in-depth look at the history and characteristics of American generations and provides context for generational differences.

Articles and Research Papers

- **"Bridging the Generation Gap & Navigating Generational Differences in the Workplace"** offers a guide to understanding and navigating generational differences in the workplace, and offers practical strategies for effective collaboration.

- **"The Impact of Cross-Cultural Communication on Organizational Citizenship Behavior in Global Virtual Teams"** is a research paper examining cross-cultural communication challenges and strategies in a globalized work environment.

Reflection Questions: Emotional Intelligence, Cultural, and Generational Differences

Understanding emotions: Consider a recent situation where you felt strong emotions like happiness, anger, sadness, etc. Write about what triggered those feelings and how you responded. How can this experience help you to understand your emotions better in the future?

Cultural connections: Reflect on a time when you interacted with someone from a different culture. What did you learn from that experience? How did it shape your understanding of their values and perspectives? What could you do differently next time to enhance that connection?

Generational differences: Consider a conversation you had with someone from a different generation. What were the key differences in your views or communication styles? How can you apply this understanding to improve your relationships with people of different ages?

Empathy in action: Write about a time when you empathized with someone in a tough situation. What did you do to show your support? How did this experience impact your emotional intelligence and ability to connect with others?

Personal growth: Consider how your cultural and generational background has shaped your beliefs and choices. What are some beliefs or biases you hold that may come from your background? How can you challenge yourself to be more open-minded and understand others' experiences?

Chapter 10:

Building Strong Relationships

I regard gratitude as an asset, and its absence a major interpersonal flaw. – Marshall Goldsmith

The more that Claire worked on developing her emotional intelligence, the more she noticed the changes in her life and her closest relationships. She understood her emotions and reactions better than ever and was starting to connect better with others. Her entire life was slowly changing for the better, and it felt like a breath of fresh air.

One of the big changes that Claire saw was with her partner, Jake. When agreements arose, instead of reacting defensively, she would pause to check in with herself. One evening, when Jake seemed distant, she did not jump to conclusions; instead, she asked, "Is everything okay?" Jake then opened up to her about his stressful day at work, and Claire realized how easily miscommunication could have led to an argument. Her empathy created an opportunity for connection instead.

Claire also saw changes in her relationships. She became a better listener, focusing on understanding rather than giving advice. When friends shared their problems with her, she would validate their feelings instead of trying to "fix things", which deepened the conversations and strengthened their bonds.

At work, Claire used her improving emotional intelligence skills to navigate these tense situations, showing empathy and staying calm. This helped to defuse conflicts and encouraged others to be more understanding. Through these experiences, Claire learned that EI was not just about managing emotions but about connecting with others and forming healthy relationships.

Healthy Relationships Under the Microscope

Healthy relationships and good communication are important for your well-being, happiness, mental health, and achievements. A healthy relationship is one where people feel emotionally safe and respected.

In a healthy relationship, you can freely express your thoughts, feelings, and vulnerabilities without fear of judgment. Mutual respect, equality, support, celebrating, and providing comfort during tough times are all essential aspects of healthy relationships.

Let's look closely at some key things that healthy relationships are built on.

Trust and Honesty

Trust means you can rely on someone; honesty means being truthful and open. In a healthy relationship, both people feel safe sharing their thoughts and feelings without fear of being lied to or betrayed.

Trust is crucial for strong relationships, providing security and stability. It allows vulnerability, respect for boundaries, and emotional well-being protection. Trust is the foundation of emotional intimacy and connection, fostering openness and mutual understanding.

When there is no trust, relationships can suffer from suspicion, fear, and emotional distance, leading to misunderstandings and conflicts. Signs of a lack of trust and honesty in a relationship include:

- frequent lying or hiding important information
- constant suspicion or jealousy, feeling the need to check on each other
- not feeling safe to share personal thoughts or concerns
- broken promises or unreliable behavior

With that said, trust issues can arise from past experiences, insecurities, or specific events within the relationship. Addressing these issues is crucial for maintaining a healthy and trusting relationship.

You can work toward rebuilding trust and honesty by:

- **Being consistent:** Follow through on promises and commitments.

- **Being transparent:** Share your feelings, thoughts, and plans openly, even when it's difficult.

- **Acknowledging your mistakes:** Admit when you're wrong and work to make things right.

- **Avoiding deception:** Be upfront and avoid hiding or distorting the truth, even in small matters.

Mutual Respect

This means truly valuing each other's opinions, feelings, and boundaries. It is about treating each other as equals and acknowledging each other's needs, even when you do not always agree.

Signs of a lack of mutual respect in a relationship include:

- disrespecting each other's opinions or belittling their feelings

- one person is trying to control or dominate decisions

- not valuing each other's time, effort, or contributions

- ignoring or dismissing boundaries or personal space

Here is how you can work toward building mutual respect:

- **Value each other's differences:** Recognize and appreciate that you both have different opinions, needs, and perspectives.

- **Practice active listening:** Listen carefully and acknowledge the other person's feelings without interrupting.

- **Encourage each other's goals:** Support each other's growth and ambitions without jealousy or competition.

- **Be considerate:** Take time to think about how your words and actions affect the other person.

Open Communication

Healthy communication is about expressing thoughts, concerns, and feelings openly and clearly. It is also about listening to the other person without judgment and ensuring that both parties feel heard.

Signs of a lack of open communication in a relationship include:

- avoiding difficult conversations, leading to unresolved issues
- one person shutting down, withdrawing, or giving the silent treatment
- frequent misunderstandings or assumptions instead of clear discussions
- not feeling heard or validated during conversations

Here is how you can work toward building open communication:

- **Create a safe space for dialogue:** Encourage open discussions without judgment or criticism.

- **Be clear and direct:** Share your thoughts and feelings honestly without expecting the other person to read your mind.

- **Ask open-ended questions:** Show genuine interest in each other's thoughts by asking questions that invite deeper conversation.

- **Stay calm during conflict:** Avoid raising your voice, and instead, focus on expressing your concerns calmly and constructively.

Empathy and Understanding

Empathy means putting yourself in the other person's shoes and understanding how they feel. It helps to build a deeper emotional connection and allows people to support each other during tough times.

Signs of a lack of empathy and understanding in a relationship include:

- dismissing the other person's feelings or concerns as unimportant

- lack of emotional support during difficult times

- jumping to conclusions or judgments instead of trying to understand the other's perspective

- not considering how your actions or words affect the other person

Here is how you can work toward building empathy and understanding:

- **Put yourself in their shoes:** Not literally, but imagine how the other person feels in difficult situations.

- **Show emotional support:** Offer a listening ear, comfort, or reassuring presence during tough times.

- **Validate their feelings:** Even if you don't fully agree, acknowledge that their emotions are real and important.

- **Practice patience:** Be patient when the other person is going through something, even if you don't fully understand it.

Healthy Boundaries

Boundaries are personal limits that help people feel comfortable and respected. Healthy relationships involve recognizing and honoring each other's space, time, and needs while maintaining a balance that works for both people.

Respecting boundaries is crucial for maintaining individuality and preventing resentment in any relationship. Personal boundaries might involve:

- how much time you need for yourself
- how you wish to be treated
- what topics are off-limits

Signs of a lack of healthy boundaries in a relationship include:

- feeling pressured to say "yes" to things that make you uncomfortable
- one person controls or intrudes on the other's personal space, time, or decisions
- guilt-tripping or manipulation when someone tries to set boundaries
- constantly feeling overwhelmed or drained due to lack of personal space

Here is how you can work toward building healthy boundaries:

- **Communicate your needs:** Be open about your limits and what you're comfortable with in the relationship.

- **Respect the other person's boundaries:** Accept and honor the boundaries your partner sets without pushing them.

- **Learn to say "no":** Don't be afraid to say no when something doesn't feel right or you need time.

- **Take time for self-care:** Make space for your well-being and encourage others to do the same.

Effective Communication Strategies

Effective communication is the cornerstone of any successful personal or professional relationship. It allows people to express their thoughts, share feelings, and resolve conflicts constructively.

Healthy relationships require communication, which can take different forms, each with nuances and importance. Verbal communication is the most direct form of communication, which involves using words to convey a message. Effective verbal communication means being able to choose and deliver the right words respectfully and appropriately. Tone, pace, and articulation all affect how your message is received.

Next, much of our communication is non-verbal and is conveyed through body language, facial expressions, gestures, and eye contact. Non-verbal cues can reinforce or contradict what is being said verbally, so it's important to be aware of them.

Then, one gets written communication. In today's digital age, written communication—like emails, texts, and social media—plays a significant role in our interactions. Written communication lacks the immediate feedback of face-to-face conversation, so clarity is even more critical. Ensuring your written messages are clear, polite, and free of ambiguity can prevent misunderstandings and maintain positive relationships.

Keys to Mastering Effective Communication

Principle	What it means	Why it matters
Active listening	Truly focusing on the speaker, absorbing what they are saying without distraction, and responding thoughtfully.	Listening is as important as speaking. It shows respect and ensures you fully understand the other person's words before responding.
Clarity and conciseness	Communicating your message in a clear, straightforward way without unnecessary details or jargon.	Being clear and to the point helps prevent confusion and ensures your message is understood quickly and easily.
Empathy	Understanding and acknowledging the feelings and perspectives of others when communicating.	Empathy fosters trust, reduces conflict, and makes the other person feel heard and valued.
Nonverbal communication	Using body language, facial expressions, tone of voice, and gestures to reinforce your words.	Nonverbal cues can often convey more than words. They add depth to your message and help others interpret your true intentions.

Being open-minded	Being willing to listen to new ideas or perspectives, even if they differ from your own.	Open-mindedness encourages a collaborative environment where all voices are heard, fostering innovation and mutual respect.
Constructive feedback	Giving feedback that is specific, respectful, and focused on improvement rather than criticism.	Constructive feedback helps people grow and improves overall communication by addressing issues in a positive, actionable way.
Adaptability	Adjusting your communication style to suit the person or situation you are engaging with.	Every individual or context may require a different approach. Being adaptable ensures that your message is effective, no matter who you speak with.
Asking questions	Seeking clarity or encouraging further explanation to understand the other person's message fully.	Questions help prevent miscommunication, clarify doubts, and show that you're genuinely engaged in the conversation.
Confidence	Speaking with assurance while maintaining respect and humility.	Confidence helps you express yourself clearly and assertively, making others more likely to listen and engage with your ideas.

Respectful language Using polite, considerate language shows regard for the other person's feelings. Respectful language helps maintain a positive atmosphere and prevents conversations from becoming arguments.

With that said, there are barriers to effective communication that can disrupt the flow of conversation, leading to misunderstandings, frustration, and conflict. These barriers include:

- lack of active listening
- language barriers
- emotional barriers
- cultural differences
- physically barriers
- assumptions and stereotyping
- interruptions
- overuse of jargon or technical language
- selective hearing or listening
- non-verbal miscommunication
- stress and overwhelm
- differences in communication styles
- lack of feedback
- prejudice or bias
- information overload

- defensiveness

- fear of judgment or rejection

To improve communication in relationships, consider the following strategies:

- active listening techniques

- I-messages vs you-messages

- open-ended questions

Effective communication is a skill that can be developed and refined over time. Remember, communication is not just about speaking; it's about creating a space where both parties feel heard, understood, and respected.

Conflict Resolution Strategies

Conflict is an inevitable part of any relationship, and it arises when two or more people have differing opinions, values, or goals. Understanding the nature of conflict is essential for managing it effectively.

Conflicts can arise in relationships for several reasons, including:

- differences in values and beliefs

- communication breakdown

- unmet needs and expectations

- stress and external pressures;

- different communication styles

- unresolved past issues

- jealousy and insecurity

- power struggles

- different coping mechanisms

- lack of quality time

- changes in life circumstances

- assumptions and misinterpretations

- personal differences

- resentment

- lack of conflict resolution skills

With that said, not all conflict is harmful. Healthy conflict allows for the expression of different viewpoints and can lead to growth and deeper understanding within a relationship. It involves respectful dialogue and focusing on resolution rather than winning the argument. On the other hand, unhealthy conflict is characterized by personal attacks, blame, and unresolved tension, which can damage the relationship over time.

To resolve conflict, it is important that you:

- **Stay calm and collected:** Managing emotions during a disagreement is crucial. When emotions are high, rational thinking can be clouded, leading to reactive and hurtful behavior. Taking a moment to breathe, gather your thoughts, and approach the situation calmly can prevent escalation.

- **Focus on the issue, not the person:** It's important to address the problem rather than attacking the other person. Personal attacks and blaming language can create defensiveness and deepen the conflict. Instead, focus on the specific issue that needs to be resolved.

- **Work together to find a solution:** A win-win solution is the goal of conflict resolution. This involves working together to find a resolution that satisfies everyone's needs. Collaborative problem-solving encourages mutual respect and cooperation, leading to more sustainable solutions.

Steps to Resolve Conflict

1. **Identify the root cause:** Understanding the underlying cause of the conflict is the first step in resolving it. This requires both parties to reflect on their feelings and needs and communicate them openly. Sometimes, what appears to be the issue on the surface may have deeper, unaddressed roots.

2. **Communicate openly:** Open and honest communication is key to resolving conflict. Both parties should express their thoughts and feelings without fear of judgment or retribution. Listening actively to each other's perspectives and validating their feelings is important, even if you disagree.

3. **Negotiate and compromise:** Conflict resolution often involves compromise. After understanding each other's needs and perspectives, work together to find a middle ground. Compromise doesn't mean one person has to give up everything; instead, it's about finding a solution that considers both parties' needs.

After resolving a conflict, forgiving and moving past any hurt or resentment is essential. Holding onto grudges can poison the relationship and lead to future conflicts. Forgiveness is a process, and it may take time, but it's a crucial step in healing.

If the conflict involves a breach of trust, taking deliberate steps to rebuild it is important. This might involve being more transparent, keeping promises, and demonstrating consistent, reliable behavior over time.

Remember that conflict can be an opportunity for growth if handled correctly. By resolving disagreements healthily, relationships can become stronger and more resilient. It allows both parties to understand each other better and develop a deeper connection based on mutual respect and understanding.

Interactive Element: Communication Skills Exercise

This exercise is a simple yet powerful way to practice and improve your communication skills, ultimately leading to stronger, more resilient relationships. It is designed to help you and your partner practice key communication techniques, like active listening and reflective responding, which are vital for healthy interactions.

Step-by-Step Guide

1. **Pair up:** Begin by finding a partner to practice with. Ideally, this should be someone you trust and feel comfortable with, as this will create a safe space for open and honest communication.

2. **Choose a topic:** Together, select a topic for your discussion. It's best to start with something neutral or a minor issue, as the exercise focuses on practicing communication skills, not resolving deep or complex conflicts.

3. **Practice active listening:** Decide who will speak first and who will listen. The speaker should share their thoughts or feelings about the chosen topic. The listener's job is to fully concentrate on what the speaker is saying, without interrupting or thinking about their response.

4. **Reflect and respond:** Once the speaker has finished, the listener reflects on what they heard. This can be done by paraphrasing the speaker's words or summarizing their main points. After reflecting, the listener can respond thoughtfully, ensuring the response is relevant and respectful.

5. **Switch roles:** After the initial round, switch roles, so the listener becomes the speaker and vice versa. Repeat the process, allowing each person to practice speaking and listening skills.

6. **Discuss and reflect:** After completing the exercise, take some time to discuss the experience with your partner. Reflect on what aspects of the exercise worked well—like feeling heard or understanding the other person's perspective better. Also, consider areas where you could improve, like staying focused while listening or expressing your thoughts more clearly.

Reflection Questions

Reflect on a recent disagreement or conflict. How did you handle the situation? Did you manage the situation well, and what could have been handled differently?

Review the communication exercise you completed. Reflect on what you discovered about your communication style. How well did you listen, express yourself, and respond to your partner's feedback?

How do you build trust in your relationships? Are there areas where you could improve? Are you a consistent, transparent, and reliable person? Are there any areas where you could improve to strengthen the trust in your relationships?

Think about your listening skills. How can you be a better listener? What techniques and practices can you adopt to enhance your ability to listen actively and empathetically? Consider things like minimizing distractions, practicing patience, and giving full attention to the speaker.

Reflect on a time when you successfully resolved a conflict. What did you do right? What strategies and approaches contributed to resolving the issue? How can you apply these techniques to future conflicts?

Chapter 11:

Emotional Intelligence at Work

When dealing with people, remember you are not dealing with creatures of logic, but with creatures of emotion. –Dale Carnegie

Claire had begun to notice the transformative impact of emotional intelligence in her work life. At the office, she had always focused on completing tasks and meeting deadlines, but now she saw the value of understanding emotions and building stronger relationships with colleagues. She realized that EI could help her navigate workplace challenges, making her more effective and fulfilled. This realization brought a new sense of purpose and satisfaction to her work.

One of the first areas where Claire applied her skills was handling workplace conflicts. Instead of avoiding tension or getting defensive, she consciously tried to understand the emotions behind the disagreements. When a coworker disagreed with her during a team meeting, she paused before reacting, asking clarifying questions, and listening to their perspective. Focusing on their concerns instead of immediately pushing back, she defused the tension and found common ground. This approach helped resolve conflicts more quickly and earned her respect for her ability to stay calm and objective.

Claire also became more attuned to her team's moods and stress levels. She noticed that some of her coworkers became visibly anxious when workloads increased, while others withdrew. Instead of overlooking these signs, Claire took the initiative to check in with them, offering support or suggesting a quick coffee break to lighten the mood. This simple gesture showed her team that she valued them as people, not just coworkers. It created a more positive work environment where people felt comfortable sharing their challenges and asking for help.

Claire's EI also enhanced her leadership skills. She tried to include quieter team members who often hesitated to speak up when leading meetings. She would ask them specific questions to draw out their ideas, creating a space where everyone's voice could be heard. This improved the quality of discussions and boosted team morale, as people felt valued and engaged.

Through this journey, Claire realized that EI wasn't just about being "nice" at work. It was about understanding the emotions that drive behavior and using that knowledge to foster collaboration and resolve issues. She developed her EI by practicing active listening, empathy, and self-awareness. As she practiced these skills, she enjoyed work more and felt a significant reduction in stress, a reassuring sign of her growing emotional intelligence.

For instance, Claire's improved EI helped her connect with a colleague who was struggling with a personal issue, leading to a more supportive work environment. It also changed how she worked with others and helped everyone work together better. This meant she could connect with her colleagues more deeply and do better at her job. It wasn't just about getting things done but creating a supportive and emotionally smart workplace where everyone could succeed.

Leading With Emotional Intelligence

Understanding and interpreting emotions have become crucial for effective leaders, top-performing team members, and CEOs. Recognizing and responding to the emotional landscape of a workplace are now integral to achieving success and fostering a positive environment.

Emotional intelligence is all about recognizing, understanding, and managing emotions. People with high EI are not only adept at handling their own emotions but also sensitive to the feelings of others. This translates to happier employees, more productive teams, and a more cohesive company culture in the workplace.

EI theories are categorized into three main models:

The Ability Model, which Peter Salovey and John Mayer developed, focuses on:

- **Perceiving emotions:** Recognizing nonverbal cues like body language and facial expressions.

- **Reasoning with emotions:** Utilizing emotions to enhance cognitive processes and decision-making.

- **Understanding emotions:** Interpreting the emotional states of others, like recognizing that someone's anger may be directed at a situation rather than at you.

- **Managing emotions:** Regulating and responding to emotions appropriately and consistently.

The Mixed Model (developed by Daniel Goleman) outlines EI through five key components (Swift, 2023). These five elements of EI work together to enhance personal and professional interactions, leading to more effective leadership, better team dynamics, and a more positive work environment.

These elements are:

- **Self-awareness**: Self-awareness involves understanding one's emotions, strengths, weaknesses, values, and goals. It includes recognizing how these factors influence decisions and interactions with others. Being self-aware means being in tune with your emotional state and how it impacts your behavior and decisions. This awareness helps you make more informed judgments and understand your actions' effects on others.

- **Self-regulation**: Self-regulation is managing and adjusting one's emotions to foster a positive outcome. It involves controlling impulsive reactions and making decisions based on reason rather than emotion. Effective self-regulation helps maintain a stable and productive work environment, even in challenging situations and promotes a balanced and thoughtful approach to problem-solving.

- **Motivation**: Motivation refers to the internal drive to achieve goals and persist in facing obstacles. It includes a strong commitment to personal and professional goals, taking initiative, and maintaining optimism and resilience. Motivated people are driven to succeed and understand that achieving goals often requires perseverance and sustained effort.

- **Empathy**: Empathy is the capacity to recognize and understand the feelings of others. In the workplace, empathy is essential for fostering team cohesion, motivation, and support. It lets you identify when colleagues need help, understand their perspectives, and build stronger relationships. Empathetic people can create a more inclusive and supportive work environment.

- **Social skills**: Social skills involve managing relationships effectively and constructively influencing others. This includes effective communication, conflict resolution, and rapport-building skills. Strong social skills help people navigate interpersonal dynamics, resolve disagreements, and collaborate more effectively with others.

The Trait Model, developed by Konstantin Vasily Petrides, describes EI as a set of emotional self-perceptions at the lower levels of personality (Pérez-González et al., 2020). It focuses on:

- **Emotional self-perception:** One's understanding and perception of their own emotions.

- **Personality framework:** Using personality traits to explore and measure EI.

EI is more than just a buzzword; it substantially benefits individuals and organizations. Studies have consistently highlighted the advantages of high EI in the workplace, revealing how it positively impacts various aspects of professional life.

- **Higher earnings**: People with high EI often enjoy higher salaries. Research indicates that those with strong EI can earn up to $29,000 more annually than their low-EI counterparts. For every percentage-point increase in EI, a person's annual salary can rise by approximately $1,300. People with high EI also experience greater job satisfaction and are less prone to burnout.

- **Increased productivity**: EI isn't only beneficial for individuals; it also enhances team performance. Teams with even a few members who exhibit high EI can experience improved cohesion and productivity. The positive influence of high-EI members can drive better overall results.

- **Enhanced efficiency**: EI contributes to workplace efficiency. When team members understand each other's emotional states and how these relate to workloads and objectives, they can work more effectively and streamline processes.

- **Improved cohesion**: High-EI individuals excel at communication, which creates a more collaborative work environment. They are adept at sharing ideas and listening to others, strengthening team unity, and enhancing workplace dynamics.

- **Increased trust**: EI fosters trust among employees. When people manage their emotions professionally and understand each other's needs and concerns, they build stronger, more reliable relationships. Managers who show empathy and appreciate their employees' emotions often enjoy better rapport with their teams.

- **Effective emotional management**: Understanding and managing one's emotions is key to EI. This self-awareness helps people better navigate their emotional highs and lows, allowing them to manage their time and workload more effectively.

- **Enhanced impulse control:** High EI helps people control their impulses and make thoughtful decisions. Awareness of one's emotional state can guide one in reacting to situations or engaging in potentially unproductive conversations.

- **Better work environment**: A workforce of emotionally intelligent employees tends to experience lower stress levels and higher morale. Respectful and harmonious interactions contribute to a stronger and more positive company culture.

- **Higher job satisfaction**: EI boosts job satisfaction by enhancing well-being, self-esteem, and positive moods while reducing negative emotions.

- **Reduced burnout**: Employees with high EI are less likely to experience burnout, as they are better equipped to manage stress and maintain emotional balance.

- **Enhanced self-awareness**: Emotionally intelligent people are aware of their strengths and weaknesses. They handle constructive feedback gracefully and use it for personal and professional growth, avoiding the defensiveness that can hinder productivity.

Examples of Emotional Intelligence in the Workplace

An emotionally intelligent workforce exhibits several key behaviors and practices that enhance effectiveness and workplace harmony. By embodying these behaviors, an emotionally intelligent team creates a supportive, adaptable, and productive workplace where everyone feels valued and empowered.

Here are some examples:

- **Improved listening skills**: Emotionally intelligent employees practice active listening. They avoid interrupting others during meetings, provide thoughtful and constructive feedback, and offer compassionate support when needed. They foster a more collaborative and respectful environment by truly hearing and understanding their colleagues.

- **Open and honest communication**: A team with high EI embraces open and honest communication. Employees welcome honest feedback from all levels and provide channels for submitting feedback without fear of retribution. This transparency nurtures an atmosphere where people feel safe to speak up and share their perspectives.

- **Adaptability and flexibility**: Emotionally intelligent employees handle change with resilience. They do not resist new ideas or processes, but instead adapt readily and find positive aspects in challenging situations. Their flexibility helps them navigate transitions smoothly and contributes to a dynamic and responsive work environment.

- **Encouraging creativity**: Workplaces that support and foster creativity often have higher EI. Such environments promote "outside the box" thinking and innovation, as employees feel free to explore new ideas without fear of judgment. This creative freedom can lead to significant advancements and problem-solving.

- **Stress relief and compassion**: An emotionally intelligent workforce incorporates stress relief practices into their daily routines, which helps build stronger relationships among team members. Compassion and empathy are evident as employees support one another, reducing stress and enhancing overall morale.

How to Improve Emotional Intelligence in the Workplace

Improving workplace emotional intelligence is feasible and beneficial. While EI development often starts on a personal level, several methods can enhance it across teams and organizations, including:

- **Training courses and workshops**: Investing in EI training programs and workshops can be highly effective. These sessions provide employees with tools and techniques to develop their emotional intelligence. Courses often cover various aspects of EI, like self-awareness, empathy, and communication skills, offering practical strategies for improvement.

- **Group activities**: Engaging in group activities to enhance EI can be educational and enjoyable. Activities like role-playing scenarios and gamification, using tools like EI card decks, can help employees practice and apply their EI skills in a controlled environment. These exercises can simulate real-world situations and provide valuable feedback.

- **Reflecting on one's emotions**: Self-awareness, a core component of EI, can be improved through personal reflection. Encouraging employees to take time to understand their emotional responses to different situations can lead to greater self-awareness. This helps people recognize their emotional triggers and patterns, which is essential for developing empathy and better interpersonal skills.

- **Developing observation skills**: Enhancing observation skills can aid in EI development. By closely observing their emotions and reactions, employees can gain insights into their behavior and responses. This helps people manage their emotions and reactions more effectively.

- **Pausing before acting**: The "three-second rule" encourages employees to pause and reflect before reacting. This brief pause allows people to consider their emotional triggers and potential responses, reducing the likelihood of impulsive decisions. Regularly practicing mindful pauses can enhance emotional regulation and decision-making.

- **Considering others' perspectives**: Encouraging employees to understand why others behave the way they do can improve empathy. Employees can better understand their colleagues' feelings and motivations by considering personal or professional reasons behind others' actions. This practice helps build stronger, more empathetic relationships in the workplace.

- **Learning from criticism:** While often challenging, criticism can be a valuable tool for improving EI. Encourage employees to view criticism as an opportunity for growth rather than a personal attack. Reflecting on constructive feedback and separating personal emotions from the critique can help people learn and improve their emotional responses. Recognizing and dismissing invalid criticism are also crucial in this process.

Lastly, remember that applying and practicing EI skills consistently are key to improvement. Encourage employees to integrate EI techniques into their daily routines and interactions. Patience and persistence are essential, as developing a strong sense of EI takes time and ongoing effort.

Chapter 12:

Emotional Intelligence in Family Life

> *Emotional Intelligence grows through perception. Look around at your present situation and observe it through the level of feeling.* –Deepak Chopra

As Claire continued to develop her emotional intelligence, she noticed a significant impact on her family life. Previously, family dynamics often felt difficult; disagreements would escalate quickly, and certain topics were avoided. However, with her improved skills, Claire approached these interactions with a new perspective, concentrating on understanding and managing emotions within her family.

One of the first changes she made was practicing active listening with her elderly parents, partner, and children. Instead of reacting defensively during disagreements, Claire took a step back and genuinely listened to their points of view, asking questions to understand their feelings. This simple shift helped diffuse tension during heated moments and created space for more meaningful conversations. Her parents, who often struggled to express their emotions openly, began to share more with her, creating a deeper sense of connection.

Claire noticed when her mother seemed stressed and quietly helped with small tasks or suggested a relaxing walk together. With her younger child, who often felt overshadowed in family discussions, Claire tried to validate their opinions and encouraged them to share their thoughts. These small but consistent acts of empathy helped her family feel more connected and valued.

As she continued applying emotional intelligence, Claire also learned to set healthy boundaries, which improved her relationship with her family. She understood that while she could offer support, it wasn't her responsibility to fix everyone's problems. By maintaining boundaries, she avoided getting overwhelmed by family drama and could remain present without feeling drained.

The biggest change came in how Claire responded to her own emotions during family conflicts. Rather than bottling up her feelings or lashing out, she practiced self-regulation techniques, like taking deep breaths or stepping away for a few minutes to calm down. This helped her approach situations with a clearer mind and express herself more effectively.

Claire's emotional intelligence transformed her family life, turning difficult interactions into opportunities for growth and deeper connection. Her empathy, open communication, and emotional management created a supportive family environment where understanding and love could thrive. It wasn't just about avoiding conflict but also about building stronger relationships built on genuine emotional connection.

The Heart of the Family

At the heart of family life is also emotional intelligence. Families come in many different forms. Today, families can include nuclear families, extended families, single-parent families, blended families, families without children, adoptive families, and same-sex families, among others.

Ideally, your safe place to fall in life should be your family. At the end of the day, your family are the people who will stand by your side, celebrate, or comfort you in your greatest triumphs and challenges.

Whatever family looks like or means to you, it is incredibly important in modern society for several reasons:

- **Emotional support:** Families provide a vital support system, offering love, encouragement, and a safe space for everyone within the family unit to express their feelings and challenges.

- **Social development:** Family dynamics shape people within the family's social skills and behaviors, influencing how they interact with others and form relationships outside the family unit.

- **Cultural transmission:** Families are the primary means through which cultural values, traditions, and beliefs are passed down from one generation to the next, preserving cultural identity.

- **Guidance and mentorship:** Parents and guardians often play critical roles in guiding children through life's complexities, teaching essential life skills and decision-making abilities.

- **Mental health:** A supportive family environment contributes significantly to mental well-being, helping people to cope with stress, anxiety, and other challenges more effectively.

- **Economic stability:** Families often pool resources for financial stability, sharing responsibilities and supporting each other during difficult economic times.

- **Child development:** A healthy family life is crucial for children's development, affecting their emotional, cognitive, and social growth and impacting their future success.

- **Community building:** Strong families contribute to stronger communities by fostering social responsibility, volunteerism, and civic engagement.

- **Resilience:** Families that work together to face challenges build resilience, teaching members how to overcome obstacles and adapt to change.

- **Quality of life:** A stable and nurturing family environment enhances the overall quality of life, leading to greater happiness and fulfillment for people and the community.

In summary, family life plays a crucial role in personal development, societal stability, and cultural continuity, making it a fundamental aspect of modern society. Just like family is important, so is EI within the family unit. EI has a profound impact on family life in several ways, including:

- **Improved communication:** High EI enhances the ability to express feelings and needs clearly, leading to more open and honest conversations among family members.

- **Conflict resolution:** Those with strong EI can navigate conflicts more effectively, facilitating discussions and finding constructive solutions without escalating tensions.

- **Empathy:** EI fosters empathy, allowing family members to better understand each other's perspectives and feelings and strengthening emotional bonds.

- **Stronger relationships:** Understanding and managing emotions contribute to deeper connections, fostering a supportive family environment where members feel valued and understood.

- **Stress management:** High EI helps people manage stress positively, which can lead to a more peaceful home atmosphere and better-coping strategies during challenging times.

- **Parenting skills:** Parents with high EI can model emotional awareness and regulation for their children, instilling important social and emotional skills that promote well-being.

- **Adaptability:** EI enhances resilience and adaptability in the face of family changes (e.g., relocation, job changes, or new family members), helping families to adjust more smoothly.

- **Increased support:** Emotionally intelligent family members are more likely to support each other during difficult times, fostering a sense of security and connection.

- **Emotional awareness:** Understanding emotions can help family members recognize and validate each other's feelings, leading to a compassionate family dynamic.

- **Promoting positive behaviors:** EI encourages positive behaviors like patience, kindness, and respect, which are essential for a harmonious family life. Overall, EI plays a critical role in nurturing healthy family relationships promoting love, understanding, and a supportive environment.

Building EI in Family Life

Building EI within a family can create a nurturing environment where everyone within the unit can thrive. Families who are emotionally intelligent stay together.

By incorporating the practices outlined below into your daily family life, EI can be nurtured, which will lead to a more cohesive, resilient, and supportive family unit. There are several ways to develop EI within your family, including:

- **Promoting open communication:** Encourage family members to express their feelings and thoughts openly. Create a safe space where everyone feels comfortable sharing their emotions without fear of judgment.

- **Modeling self-awareness**: Parents and guardians can demonstrate self-awareness by recognizing and discussing their own emotions, which teaches children to understand their feelings, too.

- **Practicing active listening**: Teach family members to listen actively and empathetically when others are speaking. This involves paying full attention, validating feelings, and responding thoughtfully.

- **Encouraging empathy**: Encourage family members to consider other people's feelings and perspectives. Discuss scenarios where they can practice putting themselves in someone else's shoes.

- **Teaching conflict resolution**: Guide the family in resolving conflicts constructively by identifying emotions, discussing underlying issues, and finding mutually agreeable solutions.

- **Giving constructive feedback:** Encourage giving and receiving feedback in a supportive manner. Discuss how to share observations without criticism and focus on behavior rather than personal attributes.

- **Practicing emotional regulation:** Teach techniques for managing emotions, like deep breathing, taking a break, or practicing mindfulness. Help family members understand that it's okay to feel emotions, but it is also important to manage them appropriately.

- **Celebrating achievements**: Recognize and celebrate each other's accomplishments, big or small. This reinforces positive emotions and builds self-esteem within the family.

- **Establishing family rituals**: Create regular family activities that strengthen bonds, like game nights, shared meals, or outings, where emotional connections can flourish.

Remember to encourage personal growth within your family. Lovingly support each family member's personal development, interests, and passions, so that you can create an environment where emotional and social growth is valued.

Parenting With Emotional Intelligence

The day you find out you will be a parent can be the most exciting and scariest day of your life. Being a parent comes with many responsibilities, and what being a parent looked like 50 years ago and what it looks like today are two entirely different things. And no, parenting books do not hold all the answers for unique family dynamics.

The world is changing so fast that it is sometimes hard to anticipate what will come next. With that said, one thing is for sure: Parenting with EI is a must. By incorporating some key principles of EI into parenting, you can nurture emotionally healthy and resilient children and create a positive family environment.

Here are key aspects every person should know about parenting with EI:

- **Understand your emotions:** Recognize and manage your own emotions as a parent. Being self-aware allows you to model emotional regulation for your children.

- **Practice empathy:** Strive to understand your child's feelings and perspectives. Empathizing helps you connect with them and respond appropriately to their needs.

- **Encourage emotional expression:** Create an environment where children feel safe to express their emotions. Encourage them to talk about their feelings and validate those emotions.

- **Model behavior:** Demonstrate EI through your actions. Children learn by observing, so show them how to handle emotions and conflicts constructively.

- **Teach problem-solving skills:** Guide children in finding solutions to emotional challenges. Encourage them to think through problems and consider various perspectives.

- **Use positive reinforcement:** Acknowledge and reinforce positive behaviors and emotions. Praise your child for their efforts in expressing feelings and handling situations well.

- **Set boundaries and expectations:** Clearly communicate the boundaries and expectations regarding behavior while understanding their emotional experiences.

- **Be mindful:** Practice mindfulness to stay present and focused during interactions with your children. This helps respond thoughtfully rather than impulsively.

- **Encourage resilience:** Teach children how to handle setbacks and disappointments. Support them in understanding that emotions are temporary and that they can overcome challenges.

- **Invest in relationships:** Prioritize quality time with your children, building strong, trusting relationships that foster open communication and emotional safety.

Navigating Family Conflicts

No matter how perfect a family is, there will be times when conflict arises. Handing conflict in the right way is important so you can maintain a healthy family life.

Armed with EI, families can create a supportive environment where conflicts are resolved constructively, leading to stronger relationships. Here are some common family conflicts that can be effectively resolved through EI:

- **Communication issues**: Misunderstandings often arise from poor communication. Using EI can help family members express their feelings clearly and listen actively.

- **Parent-child conflicts**: Differences in opinions on discipline, independence, or lifestyle choices can lead to tension. EI allows parents to empathize with their children's perspectives while communicating their own.

- **Sibling rivalry**: Competition and jealousy among siblings can create conflicts. EI helps siblings understand each other's feelings and find ways to cooperate and support one another.

- **Role conflicts**: Conflicts may occur when family members feel their roles or responsibilities are unclear or unfair. EI can facilitate open discussions about expectations and needs.

- **Life transitions**: Events like divorce, moving, or death in a family can create emotional turmoil. EI helps family members support each other through these transitions.

- **Financial disagreements**: Money management can be a significant source of conflict. EI allows family members to discuss financial goals and concerns empathetically.

- **Cultural or generational differences**: Different values or lifestyles between generations can lead to misunderstandings. EI encourages respectful dialogue and appreciation of differing viewpoints.

- **Stress and emotional baggage**: Individual stress or past grievances can affect family dynamics. EI helps family members recognize their own emotions and those of others, fostering understanding and patience.

- **Disagreements over family traditions**: Conflicts may arise when family members have different ideas about traditions or celebrations. EI can help mediate these discussions and find common ground.

- **Resentment and unresolved conflicts**: Past grievances can lead to ongoing tension. EI aids in addressing these issues openly, promoting healing and reconciliation.

Remember that by leveraging EI, you can navigate family conflicts with greater understanding, respect, and effectiveness, ultimately strengthening familial relationships rather than destroying them. Here are examples of how EI can help you navigate family conflict:

- **Self-regulation:** When tensions rise, a person with high EI can take a step back to calm down before responding. For instance, instead of reacting harshly during an argument, they may choose to take a deep breath and express their feelings more calmly.

- **Active listening:** EI promotes active listening, allowing family members to feel heard. For example, during a disagreement, one person might ask the other to explain their perspective, demonstrating empathy and understanding.

- **Empathy:** Understanding the emotions and feelings of others can help de-escalate conflicts. A family member might say, "I see that you're upset about this situation, and I want to understand how you're feeling," which demonstrates empathy and openness.

- **Effective communication:** High EI encourages clear and respectful communication. For instance, instead of blaming, a person might use "I" statements like, "I feel hurt when you say that" instead of "You always make me feel bad."

- **Problem-solving:** Emotionally intelligent people can work collaboratively to find solutions. For example, when disagreements arise over household responsibilities, they might sit down together to discuss and negotiate a fair division of tasks.

- **Seeking compromise:** Understanding that family members may have differing viewpoints, a person with high EI might suggest a compromise, like rotating responsibilities or finding a middle ground in a decision-making process.

- **Recognizing triggers:** When you and your family can identify personal emotional triggers and those of family members, this will help them anticipate potential conflicts and address them proactively. For example, they might avoid sensitive topics during family gatherings to prevent flare-ups.

- **Taking responsibility:** When at fault, emotionally intelligent people are willing to apologize sincerely and take responsibility for their actions, which can diffuse tension and promote healing.

- **Modeling resilience:** During conflicts, emotionally intelligent people can demonstrate resilience by focusing on solutions rather than dwelling on problems, encouraging the family to move forward together.

- **Reassurance:** Offering reassurance and support to family members during conflicts helps maintain bonds. For instance, acknowledging the importance of family relationships and expressing a desire to work through issues together fosters a sense of unity.

Family Dynamics Exercise: Emotional Check-In Circle

Here's a family dynamics exercise designed to enhance EI within the family. This exercise aims to improve emotional awareness, communication, empathy, and conflict resolution within your family.

Duration: 30–45 minutes

You will need:

A comfortable space for sitting in a circle

A "talking object" (an item that can be passed around, like a soft toy or a special family item)

Step-by-step instructions:

1. Create a safe environment: Explain the purpose of the activity to enhance EI and communication within the family. For instance, set ground rules like no interrupting, no judgment, and respect for everyone's feelings and opinions.

2. Begin with an emotional check-in: Pass the talking object around the circle. Each family member takes turns holding the object and sharing their current emotional state. Encourage everyone to describe their feelings using simple terms (happy,

sad, frustrated, etc.) and, if comfortable, to share why they feel that way.

3. Share experiences: After everyone has shared their current emotions, invite each family member to discuss a recent situation where they felt their emotions were particularly strong. Ask them to explain what happened, how it made them feel, and how they dealt with those emotions.

4. Practice empathy: Once everyone has shared, ask family members to reflect on what they heard. Each person can express empathy by acknowledging or validating the feelings expressed by others. Encourage family members to respond with phrases like, "I understand why you felt that way" or "That sounds really tough."

5. Discuss conflict scenarios: Identify a past family conflict or a common trigger for disagreements. Discuss it openly, focusing on how emotions played a role in that situation. Ask family members how EI could have helped resolve that conflict better.

6. Problem-solving: As a family, brainstorm strategies for better managing emotions and conflicts in the future. Write down practical solutions everyone agrees upon, like regular family meetings or check-ins.

7. Commitment to change: Encourage each family member to express one commitment or action they will take to improve EI within the family (e.g., actively listening, using "I" statements, or practicing mindfulness). Write these commitments down and revisit them in a future family meeting.

8. Closing reflection: End the exercise by passing the talking object one last time. Each family member can share one positive takeaway from the exercise.

9. Follow-up: Consider scheduling regular check-ins (weekly or monthly) to continue building on EI, discussing feelings, and resolving any arising conflicts proactively.

Reflection Questions: Applying Emotional Intelligence in Family Relationships

Self-awareness: What emotions do I typically experience during family interactions, and how do those emotions affect my behavior and communication with family members?

Empathy: How can I better understand the feelings and perspectives of my family members, and what steps can I take to show them that I value their emotions?

Conflict resolution: How do I usually respond when conflicts arise in my family, and what EI strategies can I implement to handle disagreements more constructively?

Communication: How can I improve my communication with family members to ensure I express my feelings clearly while listening actively to their concerns?

Support and growth: How can I foster an emotionally supportive environment at home that encourages my family members to express their emotions freely and develop their own EI?

Chapter 13:

Overcoming Common Emotional Intelligence Challenges

> *In a very real sense, we have two minds, one that thinks and one that feels.* –
> Daniel Goleman

Early on in her journey with emotional intelligence, she learned that it would not all be smooth sailing. Sure, she'd made progress, but she still faced many bumps in the road.

Claire's first big challenge was handling criticism without taking it personally. For example, one day at work, her manager gave her feedback on a project that didn't exactly go as planned.

The old Claire would've immediately felt defensive or hurt, but she took a deep breath and reminded herself of what she'd been practicing. *This isn't an attack; it's a chance to improve,* she thought. Even though she could feel the sting, she listened, asking questions to understand what went wrong instead of getting caught up in her emotions. It wasn't easy, but with each feedback, she felt herself growing thicker skin and a clearer sense of where to improve.

Emotional exhaustion was the second challenge that Claire faced. Sometimes, she felt tired from the constant effort of understanding and managing her feelings. It became overwhelming to analyze her reactions and stay calm in stressful situations. To regain balance, she began setting boundaries. She realized it was okay not to overthink everything some days, allowing herself to feel without needing to solve anything.

Another hurdle was managing other people's emotions. With greater awareness of her own feelings, Claire became more sensitive to others' emotions, sometimes too sensitive. She often absorbed their stress and frustration. Over time, she realized empathy didn't mean she had to take on everyone else's feelings. She learned to recognize when someone else's mood impacted her and practiced setting a mental boundary, reminding herself, "Their feelings are theirs; mine are mine."

As Claire faced each challenge, she understood that emotional intelligence wasn't about being perfect or always having the right answer. It was about navigating emotions with curiosity and compassion, even when things got messy. Each hurdle she overcame made her stronger, wiser, and more confident.

Understanding Emotional Intelligence Challenges

Developing emotional intelligence can be an exciting journey, but many people encounter challenges along the way. This chapter will explore common EI challenges, including

- lack of self-awareness
- improving emotional awareness
- developing empathy
- social skills enhancement
- motivation and persistence
- leveraging resources and support
- sustaining progress

Lack of Self-Awareness

One common challenge is a lack of self-awareness. Without understanding your own emotions, it's difficult to manage them effectively. For instance, if you often feel anger but are not fully aware of it, you might react impulsively in situations where you should take a moment to think.

A good first step to increase self-awareness is to regularly check in with yourself. You can do this by setting aside a few minutes each day to reflect on your feelings. Ask yourself questions like, "What did I feel today?" or "How did my emotions affect my actions?"

Building Self-Awareness

Journaling can be beneficial for enhancing self-awareness. Write about your daily experiences and how they made you feel. Over time, this practice will help you identify patterns in your emotions. For example, if you notice that you often feel anxious before meetings, you can start looking into specific triggers and think of ways to manage that anxiety.

Another useful technique is mindfulness meditation. By practicing mindfulness, you become more attuned to your thoughts and feelings in the present moment. This skill allows you to recognize your emotional responses without judgment.

Improving Emotional Regulation

Another challenge in developing emotional intelligence is emotional regulation. People often struggle to control their emotions, leading to outbursts or withdrawal. For instance, you might feel overwhelmed at work and lash out at a coworker. To better manage your emotions, developing techniques for calming yourself is essential.

Deep breathing exercises can be a great way to achieve this. When you feel a strong emotional response, take a moment to breathe deeply. Inhale for a count of four, hold for four, and exhale for four. Doing this simple practice can help you regain composure and respond more thoughtfully.

Developing Empathy

Empathy is an important part of emotional intelligence, but many people find it challenging to see things from another person's perspective. You might struggle to understand why a friend is upset and instead judge their feelings. To cultivate empathy, practice active listening. This involves fully focusing on the speaker without interrupting. When someone shares their thoughts, pay attention to their words and emotions. Reflect back on what they say, like, "It sounds like you're feeling overwhelmed." This practice not only shows that you care but also helps you understand their viewpoint better.

Social Skills Enhancement

Another significant challenge is developing strong social skills. Many people feel awkward in social situations, leading them to avoid interactions altogether. To improve your social skills, start with one-on-one conversations. Begin by asking open-ended questions about the other person's interests. For example, instead of asking if they had a good weekend, you could ask what they enjoyed most about it. This approach encourages deeper conversations and can help you feel more comfortable over time. Practicing small talk can also be useful. Try greeting your neighbors or making small comments to cashiers. These small interactions can build your confidence.

Motivation and Persistence

Motivation is another area where people may struggle. Emotional intelligence requires a commitment to self-improvement, which can seem daunting. Set small, achievable goals for yourself. Instead of aiming to be entirely emotionally aware overnight, focus on one aspect at a time, like regulating anger. Establish daily reminders or set a specific time each week to focus on that goal. Celebrate your progress, no matter how small. If you successfully manage an emotional response at work one day, take a moment to acknowledge that victory. Each small win will motivate you to keep going.

Resources and Support

One often overlooked challenge is the lack of resources or support when working to develop emotional intelligence. It can feel isolating to work on these skills alone. Seek out resources that can help you. Books on emotional intelligence or workshops in your community can offer valuable insights. Additionally, consider talking to a therapist or coach who specializes in emotional intelligence. They can provide personalized strategies and support you in your journey. Connecting with others who are also working on developing their EI can create a sense of community and accountability.

Sustaining Progress

Finally, sustaining progress can be a challenge. After putting in effort, it's easy to fall back into old habits. To maintain your emotional growth, regularly revisit your goals. Create a checklist of the skills you want to improve and mark your accomplishments. Support from friends or a community group can also help reinforce your progress. Share your goals with others so they can encourage you. It's beneficial to have a network that shares their experiences, too. Discussing challenges and successes can inspire you to keep pushing forward.

Daily Reflection Journaling Exercise: Overcoming Emotional Intelligence Challenges

Here's a simple exercise you can try to develop your emotional intelligence despite any challenges you might face. Completing this exercise can enhance your self-awareness and help you manage your emotions more effectively.

This exercise aims to enhance your EI by cultivating self-awareness, understanding your emotions, and developing more effective responses to emotional situations.

You will need:

- notebook or digital document for journaling
- pen or typing device

Instructions:

1. **Set aside time:** Choose a specific time each day (preferably in the evening) to sit quietly and reflect. Remember that consistency is key.

2. **Create a comfortable environment:** Find a quiet space where you feel relaxed and free from distractions. This could be a cozy corner in your home, a coffee shop, or a park.

3. **Identify your emotions:** Reflect on your day and write down three specific emotions you felt. Be descriptive. Instead of general terms such as "happy" or "sad," try using more nuanced words: For example, "happy" could be broken down to "joyful" for a shared success or "content" for a peaceful moment. Use emotional vocabulary lists if needed to help articulate your feelings.

4. **Contextualize:** For each emotion, describe the situation that triggered it: Who was involved? (e.g., coworkers, friends, family), What happened? (e.g., a compliment received, a disagreement), How did you feel at that moment? (e.g., "I felt excited when my manager praised my project.")

5. **Evaluate your reactions:** Reflect on how you reacted to each emotion: Did you express your feelings openly to others or keep them to yourself? Were your reactions appropriate to the situation? (e.g., did you lash out in anger or respond calmly?. Note your physical reactions—did your heart race or stomach churn?

6. **Consider alternatives:** For each situation, think about how you could have responded differently: What would a more emotionally intelligent reaction look like? Write down a few examples of alternative responses. For example, instead of withdrawing during a disagreement, you might say, "I see your point, but I feel differently because..."

7. **Set intentions:** Make a commitment for the following day based on your reflections: Whether it's practicing active listening, expressing your feelings more openly, or managing stress more effectively—be specific. Example: "Tomorrow, I will actively listen to my colleague's feedback before responding, ensuring I acknowledge their perspective."

8. **Repeat:** Continue this exercise daily, updating and refining your emotions and responses as you grow. At the end of each week, review your entries to identify patterns. Observe any changes in your emotional responses and the effectiveness of your reactions over time.

Additional tips:

- Be honest in your reflections; this is for your personal growth.

- Don't rush the process—take your time to understand your emotions and responses.

- Discuss your insights with a trusted friend or mentor for further growth.

By engaging in this daily practice, you will develop greater emotional awareness, improve your ability to manage your feelings and enhance your capacity for empathy and effective communication with others.

Reflection Questions: Overcoming Challenges

What emotions do you find most difficult to understand or express, and what situations tend to trigger them?

Think of a recent conflict or disagreement. What role did your emotions play in that situation, and how could you have handled it differently?

Reflect on a time when you felt misunderstood by someone. What were the feelings involved, and how could you have communicated more effectively?

What are some recurring patterns or behaviors you notice in your interactions with others that may be hindering your ability to connect empathetically?

Consider a moment when you felt overwhelmed by your emotions. What coping strategies did you use, and how effective were they in helping you manage the situation?

Use these prompts to explore your thoughts and feelings, which can lead to greater self-awareness and emotional growth.

Be encouraged and know that navigating the journey of developing emotional intelligence comes with various challenges. By focusing on self-awareness, emotional regulation, empathy, social skills, motivation, and support, you can overcome these hurdles. Taking the time to practice these skills and to reflect on your emotional growth will empower you to lead a more emotionally intelligent life where you can not only survive in society but thrive.

It is important to remember that EI is not a destination but a continuous journey of self-discovery and improvement. Each step that you take towards understanding your emotions and the emotions of others builds a greater foundation for meaningful connections and effective communication.

Continue to work on developing your EI and embrace the setbacks as opportunities for growth; they are just as crucial to your development as the successes. As you cultivate these skills, remember that EI can significantly enhance your personal and professional relationships. It allows you to navigate conflicts more effectively, build stronger bonds with those around you, and create a positive environment that fosters collaboration and understanding.

Consider seeking resources like books, workshops, or online courses to further deepen your understanding of emotional intelligence. Surround yourself with people and content who inspire you and challenge you to grow, as their perspectives can enrich your journey.

In moments when self-doubt creeps in, remind yourself of the progress you've made. Always celebrate small victories along the way, whether it's recognizing a negative emotional response and choosing to respond thoughtfully instead, or successfully empathizing with a friend in need. Each of these moments is a testament to your commitment to growth.

Ultimately, the goal of developing EI is not only to improve your relationship with yourself, but also to positively impact those around you. By leading and living with empathy and understanding, you contribute to a more compassionate world. So, boldly choose to embrace this journey with open arms and an open heart, knowing that every effort counts. Strive for progress, not perfection, and watch as you flourish in all areas of your life.

Chapter 14:

Planning for On-Going Growth

There is nothing noble in being superior to your fellow man; true nobility is being superior to your former self. –Ernest Hemingway

Claire had come far on her emotional intelligence journey, and looking back on her progress, she realized that this wasn't something she could "finish" and check off a to-do list. EI wasn't a goal with an endpoint but a lifelong journey. And that was okay.

With this new perspective and not wanting to fall back into old habits, Claire mapped a plan for continued growth. She set some simple, realistic goals that would help keep her on track without overwhelming her.

First, she committed to daily check-ins with herself. Just five minutes a day to sit quietly, reflect on her emotions, and notice if there were any patterns she needed to address. Some days, it was as simple as asking, *How am I feeling today, and why?* On other days, it led to deeper insights, like recognizing that she was letting small stressors build up or that she'd been neglecting self-care.

Next, Claire made continuous learning a priority. She decided to read one new book about EI or self-growth every couple of months and listen to podcasts during her commute. It wasn't just about adding new tools to her emotional toolkit, but about staying inspired and reminding herself that growth is an ongoing process.

To practice her skills in real-life situations, she also set a goal to step out of her comfort zone at least once a month. Whether that meant having a tough conversation she'd been avoiding, trying something new that scared her a little, or even just putting herself out there more socially, these small challenges kept her pushing forward.

Lastly, Claire wanted to find a way to give back. The impact of learning about EI had been so profound for her that she felt a growing desire to share what she'd learned with others. She started small—chatting with friends about what she was learning, suggesting books, or practicing active listening more intently when people opened up to her. She figured that by helping others on their journeys, she'd continue growing on hers.

Claire didn't have everything figured out and knew there'd be setbacks along the way. But with a clear plan and the understanding that personal growth was a lifelong commitment, she felt ready to confidently and calmly face whatever came next.

An Ongoing Journey

As you have faithfully worked through this book, you have already learned much about emotional intelligence. With that said, your journey with EI will be ongoing, as there is always more to learn. Be committed to your personal growth and keep working toward your growth.

EI is essential for daily life. It involves understanding and managing your feelings while also recognizing and influencing the feelings of others. In this book, you've gained insight into your emotions, learned to empathize with others, and discovered strategies for navigating social interactions more effectively. Remember, acquiring knowledge about EI is merely the first step in your journey.

Commitment to Personal Growth

To develop your emotional intelligence, you must commit to continuous personal growth. This commitment involves setting aside time to reflect on your emotions and how they influence your thoughts and actions. Practice keeping a journal to record your emotional experiences and reactions in different situations. Writing down your feelings will help you process them more effectively and bring clarity to your experiences.

You can also set specific goals to improve your emotional skills. For instance, you might aim to practice empathy by actively listening to others without interrupting. You could also focus on managing your stress responses in challenging situations by using techniques like deep breathing or mindfulness. By establishing clear goals, you map out a path for your ongoing growth.

Building on Your Knowledge

As you move forward, continue building on the knowledge you have gained. Consider revisiting key concepts from this book by summarizing them in your own words. Doing this will reinforce your understanding and make the information more accessible for future reference. You can even discuss these concepts with friends or family to better understand EI within your social circles.

Resources like articles, podcasts, or workshops can also offer fresh perspectives and insights. Look for materials that suit your learning style and interests. For example, if you enjoy listening to stories, find podcasts that discuss EI. Engaging with diverse sources of information will stimulate your curiosity and enhance your growth.

Real-Life Application

EI is not just a theoretical concept; it must be applied in real life. Pay attention to your daily interactions. Observe your emotional responses and consider what drives them. Recognizing triggers can help you manage your reactions more effectively. For example, if you notice that you tend to feel overwhelmed during team meetings, you might choose to prepare beforehand or practice techniques to remain calm.

Another practical approach is to enhance your communication skills. Use "I" statements to express your feelings constructively. Instead of saying, "You make me feel frustrated," try rephrasing it as "I feel frustrated when things don't go as planned." This shift encourages open dialogue and reduces defensiveness, enhancing interpersonal relationships.

Practicing Empathy

Empathy is a core component of emotional intelligence. To develop empathy, you can practice putting yourself in others' shoes. When someone shares a problem or expresses a feeling, take a moment to consider how you would feel in their situation. By connecting with their emotions, you demonstrate understanding and compassion.

To cultivate empathy further, try asking open-ended questions during conversations. Questions like, "How did that situation make you feel?" invite the other person to share their thoughts and emotions. This deepens your connection and enhances your ability to interpret others' emotional cues.

Handling Difficult Emotions

You'll encounter difficult emotions like anger, sadness, or frustration on your journey. It's crucial to approach these feelings constructively. Instead of letting them dictate your behavior, identify healthy coping strategies.

One effective technique is recognizing thoughts that trigger negative emotions. You can reduce their emotional impact by challenging these thoughts—asking yourself if they are rational or exaggerated.

When you feel overwhelmed, take breaks to regroup. Engage in activities you enjoy or use relaxation techniques to soothe your mind. Regular physical activity is also a powerful way to manage emotions. Exercise releases endorphins, promoting a positive mindset. Even a short walk can help clear your thoughts and regain focus.

Encouraging Supportive Environments

Building a supportive environment can boost your emotional intelligence. Surround yourself with people who inspire you and make you feel good. Find friends who communicate openly and share their feelings. When you feel safe to express yourself, you'll grow emotionally.

At work, create a peer support group where colleagues can share experiences and offer feedback on emotional struggles. This initiative fosters community and joint development. Participating in activities that build trust helps team members bond more deeply, boosting EI within the workplace.

Lifelong Learning

Continually assess your emotional strengths and areas for improvement. Include regular self-reflections in your routine to evaluate your progress. As you gain more experience, you might find new ways to apply EI in various settings, enriching your personal and professional interactions. Your enhanced emotional understanding can benefit board meetings, family gatherings, or casual encounters.

Celebrating Progress

As you navigate this journey, it's important to celebrate your progress. Acknowledging your achievements—no matter how small—builds confidence and motivates further growth. Consider creating a visual reminder of your goals and milestones to keep them in mind and inspire you along the way.

Sharing your growth journey with friends or family can also provide encouragement and accountability. When you involve others, you reinforce your commitment and inspire them to embark on their own journeys of emotional intelligence.

Step-by-Step Plan for Ongoing Growth

Here's an in-depth plan to help develop self-awareness. This plan can significantly improve self-awareness, enhancing your emotional intelligence and interpersonal relationships.

1. Set intentions.

- **Goal setting:** Define specific self-awareness goals. For instance, aim to understand your emotional triggers or identify your core values.

- **Time frame:** Set a timeline (e.g., three months) to evaluate your progress.

2. Practice mindfulness.

- **Daily meditation:** Dedicate 5–10 minutes daily to mindfulness meditation. Focus on your breath and observe your thoughts without judgment.

- **Body scan:** Engage in body scan exercises to become aware of physical sensations and emotional responses.

3. Keep a journal.

- **Emotional check-ins:** Daily or weekly, write about your emotions, thoughts, and events that triggered specific feelings.

- **Patterns and triggers:** Regularly review your entries to identify recurring themes or patterns in your behavior.

4. Seek feedback.

- **Trusted individuals:** Select a few trusted friends, family members, or colleagues and ask for honest feedback about your strengths and areas for improvement.

- **Constructive criticism:** Approach feedback with an open mind and reflect on how you can incorporate it into your personal growth.

5. **Engage in self-reflection.**
    - **End-of-day reflection:** Spend a few minutes each evening reflecting on your day. Consider moments when you felt particularly strong emotions and analyze why.
    - **Prompts:** Use self-reflection prompts, like "What did I learn about myself today?" or "What made me feel uncomfortable?"

6. **Explore your values and beliefs.**
    - **Values assessment:** Create a list of your core values. Consider what matters most to you, like family, integrity, or creativity.
    - **Align actions with values:** Regularly evaluate how your actions align with your values and make adjustments where necessary.

7. **Practice active listening.**
    - **Focus on others:** During conversations, concentrate on truly listening instead of formulating your response.
    - **Reflect:** After someone shares, reflect back on what you heard to ensure understanding and build a connection.

8. **Regular check-ins.**
    - **Weekly reviews:** Schedule a dedicated time each week to review your self-awareness journey, assess your progress, and adjust your strategies as needed.
    - **Accountability:** Share your goals with someone who can help keep you accountable and provide support.

9. **Experiment with new experiences**.
   - **Challenge yourself:** Step outside your comfort zone by trying new activities or pursuing challenging interests.
   - **Learn from failure:** Embrace mistakes and analyze what you can learn to enhance your understanding of yourself.

10. **Educate yourself**.
    - **Read books and articles:** Explore resources on emotional intelligence and self-awareness. Consider titles like *Emotional Intelligence* by Daniel Goleman.
    - **Attend workshops:** Look for webinars, workshops, or courses focusing on emotional intelligence and self-awareness development.

Weekly Activity Planner: Increased Emotional Intelligence

Here is a weekly activity planner that you can use to continue building emotional intelligence. Remember that all the effort you put into personal development will pay off. You can enhance your emotional intelligence by incorporating small yet consistent actions into your daily routine.

Monday: Self-Reflection

Start your week with self-reflection. Spend at least 15 minutes reviewing your previous week. Think about your feelings during specific situations. Note any moments when you felt particularly happy, stressed, or confused. Reflecting on these emotions can help you recognize patterns in how you respond to different situations. For example, if you often feel anxious during meetings, this awareness is the first step in addressing that anxiety.

You can create a simple journal or digital document for this purpose. Write down the date, emotion, situation, and your response. This will become a useful tool for tracking your emotional responses over time.

Tuesday: Journaling

On Tuesdays, dedicate time to journaling about your emotions. Pick a quiet spot and write freely about what you are feeling. Start with a prompt like "Today, I felt ___ because ___." This practice allows you to express your thoughts without judgment. It provides clarity on your feelings and helps you release any pent-up emotions.

Set a timer for 20 minutes and write continuously. Don't worry about grammar or punctuation; just let your thoughts flow. After writing, take a moment to read what you've written. Highlight any key emotions or themes that stand out to you.

Wednesday: Active Listening

Wednesday is all about practicing active listening. During conversations with others, focus entirely on what they are saying. Avoid interrupting or planning your response while they are talking. Instead, listen carefully and show your understanding through body language, such as nodding or maintaining eye contact.

After they finish speaking, summarize what they said to ensure you understood them correctly. This shows that you value their words and helps you develop empathy. For instance, if a friend shares a problem, you could respond with, "It sounds like you are feeling overwhelmed about that situation." This validates their feelings and encourages a deeper connection.

Thursday: Expressing Gratitude

Take time on Thursdays to express gratitude. Write down three people in your life who have positively impacted you. Reach out to them with a message or a call, and tell them why you appreciate them. This practice boosts your mood and can enhance your relationships.

Gratitude can take many forms. You might send a handwritten note, a text message, or even a heartfelt email. For example, if a coworker helped you with a project, you could say, "I really appreciated your help on the project last week. It made a significant difference." This not only acknowledges their effort but also strengthens your bond.

Friday: Mindfulness Practice

Fridays are for mindfulness practice. Set aside at least 10 minutes to engage in mindfulness activities. This could include meditation, deep breathing exercises, or even just sitting quietly and focusing on your surroundings. Mindfulness helps you stay present and can reduce stress.

You can start with guided meditation available on various apps. For example, try a simple deep-breathing exercise: Inhale deeply for four seconds, hold your breath for four, and exhale for four. Repeat this cycle several times, and notice how your body feels. This practice can enhance your self-awareness, making it easier to manage your emotions.

Saturday: Social Interaction

On weekends, focus on social interaction. Spend time with friends or family, or even make new connections. Engage in meaningful conversations where you can share feelings and learn about others. This helps in building empathy and social awareness.

You might plan a casual meetup, a coffee date, or even a phone call with someone you haven't spoken to in a while. When you meet, ask open-ended questions like, "How have you been feeling lately?" This encourages deeper dialogue and shows that you care, fostering emotional bonds.

Sunday: Goal Setting

As your week comes to an end, spend Sundays setting emotional intelligence goals for the coming week. Reflect on what you learned about yourself and others throughout the week. From your journaling and social interactions, identify areas where you can improve. Set one or two specific, measurable goals for the week.

For example, if you noticed that you struggle to manage stress, you might set a goal to practice mindfulness twice during the coming week. Writing down these goals in a dedicated space can help you stay accountable. Check in on your progress as the week unfolds.

Implementing this weekly activity planner can significantly impact your emotional intelligence. By dedicating time to self-reflection, journaling, listening, expressing gratitude, practicing mindfulness, socializing, and setting goals, you will notice improvements over time. Consistency is key; the more you invest in these practices, the more positive changes you will experience in your emotional awareness and management.

Reflection Questions: Ongoing Growth

How has your understanding of your emotions deepened over the past few weeks, and how has this impacted your interactions with others?

What new strategies or techniques have you implemented recently to manage your emotions, and how effective have they been in different situations?

Reflect on a recent conversation where you practiced active listening. How did this change the dynamics of the interaction, and what did you learn from it?

What challenges have you faced in your emotional intelligence journey, and how have you navigated these challenges to continue your growth?

Think about someone whom you deeply respect for their emotional intelligence. What qualities do they possess, and how can you incorporate similar traits into your own life?

Conclusion

One can choose to go back toward safety or forward toward growth. Growth must be chosen again and again; fear must be overcome again and again. –Abraham Maslow

As you come to the end of this exploration of emotional intelligence, reflect on the profound impact of this powerful tool. EI is not merely a concept confined to this book; it is a way of being that can transform your relationships, enhance your decision-making, and empower you to navigate life with grace and resilience.

Throughout your journey, you discovered the core components of EI: self-awareness, self-regulation, empathy, social skills, and motivation. These elements serve as building blocks, creating a strong foundation for understanding yourself and connecting with others. The time has come to integrate these lessons into your daily life and empower yourself and others.

Self-awareness is the cornerstone of EI. By developing an acute awareness of your emotions, strengths, weaknesses, values, and motivations, you unlock the door to self-discovery. This awareness lets you see yourself clearly, acknowledging your flaws while celebrating your successes. As you move forward, commit to continuous self-reflection. Consider journaling your thoughts and feelings, meditating, or seeking feedback from trusted friends. Doing this will deepen your understanding and guide you toward more authentic living.

Remember that managing your emotions, especially in challenging situations, is vital to EI. Self-regulation equips you with the tools to pause, reflect, and respond well rather than react impulsively. Imagine navigating conflicts with composure, responding to stressors calmly, and making decisions based on thoughtful consideration rather than emotional turmoil. Strive to practice mindfulness, recognize your emotional triggers, and employ techniques like deep breathing or visualization to regain control of intense moments. Remember, mastery over your emotions does not mean suppressing them; rather, it involves understanding and channeling them constructively.

At the heart of EI, empathy helps you forge deep connections with others. Empathy becomes a bridge of understanding and compassion in a world that can feel fragmented and isolated. Challenge yourself to listen actively to others, to put yourself in their shoes, and to validate their feelings. When you approach conversations empathetically, you cultivate a culture of trust and openness. Doing this strengthens your relationships and enriches your emotional landscape, allowing you to experience the joy of shared human experiences.

Whether at work, at home, or within your community—effective social skills are crucial. They help you to communicate clearly, resolve conflicts, and collaborate. As you move forward, prioritize the development of these skills. Engage in meaningful conversations, practice assertiveness, and learn to navigate difficult discussions tactfully and respectfully. Embrace the human experience, recognizing that each person has a unique perspective to share. By honing your social skills, you will enhance your relationships and create a positive ripple effect in your community.

Intrinsic motivation is a driving force behind EI, it pushes you to pursue your passions, set meaningful goals, and strive for personal growth. As you reflect on your journey thus far, consider what ignites your passion. What are your core values, and how can you align your actions with them? Set goals that inspire you and break them down into manageable steps. Celebrate your achievements, no matter how small, and remember that the path to success is often a winding road filled with learning experiences. Embrace a growth mindset—understanding that failures are not setbacks but growth opportunities.

Resilience is a vital outcome of EI. Life is filled with challenges, disappointments, and setbacks. However, how you respond to these adversities defines your character and shapes your future. As you cultivate EI, you will develop a resilient mindset, enabling you to face difficulties with courage and perseverance. Embrace challenges as opportunities to learn and grow, and remind yourself that it is okay to ask for help when needed. Surround yourself with supportive people who uplift and inspire you. Together, you can build a resilient community that thrives in adversity.

As you continue to embrace EI, remember it is not solely an individual endeavor but a collective one. Strive to create a culture of EI in your family, workplace, and community. Share your insights, engage in open dialogues about emotions, and encourage others to embrace the principles you have learned. You contribute to a world where empathy, understanding, and connection flourish by fostering an environment that values EI.

Last but not least, take the knowledge and insights that you have gained from this book and apply them in your life. Remember, EI is an ongoing journey, a lifelong commitment to growth and self-discovery. Embrace the beauty of being human—the complexities, the emotions, the connections. Remember, you can shape your reality, influence those around you, and contribute positively to the world.

My Emotional Intelligence Notes

My Emotional Intelligence Notes

My Emotional Intelligence Notes

References

Akene, E. (2020, October 13). *The chemistry behind our emotions*. Medium. https://ericaakene.medium.com/the-chemistry-behind-our-emotions-2eaf9aaf82f6

Brach, T. (2024). *Radical acceptance*. Penguin Random House Canada. https://www.penguinrandomhouse.ca/books/16998/radical-acceptance-by-tara-brach-phd/9780553380996

Bridging the gap & navigating generational differences in the workplace. (2024, June 13). The AR Group, LLC. https://theargroup.com/blog/bridging-the-gap-navigating-generational-differences-in-the-workplace/

Building your resilience. (2020, February 1). American Psychological Association. https://www.apa.org/topics/resilience/building-your-resilience

Cherry, MSEd, K. (2018). *Report Viewer | Woodcock-Johnson 111 test of cognitive abilities*. Common Data Elements. https://www.commondataelements.ninds.nih.gov/report-viewer/23955/Woodcock-Johnson%20III%20Test%20of%20Cognitive%20Abilities

Cherry, K. (2022). *How does the Weschsler adult intelligence scale measure intelligence?* Verywell Mind. https://www.verywellmind.com/the-wechsler-adult-intelligence-scale-2795283

Cherry, K. (2023, December 31). *5 Key components of emotional intelligence*. Verywell Mind. https://www.verywellmind.com/components-of-emotional-intelligence-2795438

Cooks-Campbell, A. (2023, August 9). *EQ versus IQ: What are they and which Is more important?* BetterUp. https://www.betterup.com/blog/eq-vs-iq

Dweck, C. S. (2007). *Mindset: The new psychology of success.* Ballantine Books.

Edis, N. (2024a, February 7). *A quote by Dale Carnegie.* ThinkPsych. https://thinkpsych.com/blogs/posts/30-best-quotes-about-emotional-intelligence?srsltid=AfmBOoq9AGFI2tFt9Q1x1lubjb0qFbcPHYcH8FxrNt-zVEZy5PO2JMEN

Emotional Intelligence Test. (n.d.). Psychology Today https://www.psychologytoday.com/za/tests/personality/emotional-intelligence-test

Empathy definition | what is empathy? (2009). Greater Good Magazine. https://greatergood.berkeley.edu/topic/empathy/definition

Erieau, C. (2019, February 20). *A quote by Angela Duckworth.* Driven App. https://home.hellodriven.com/articles/the-50-best-resilience-quotes/

Extrinsic & Intrinsic Motivation examples - What's the difference? (2020, February 2). SprigghHR. https://sprigghr.com/blog/hr-professionals/extrinsic-intrinsic-motivation-examples-whats-the-difference/

Goleman, D. (2019). *Emotional intelligence: Why it can matter more than IQ.* Random House Publishing Group.

Hanson, R. (2024). *Resilient: How to grow an unshakable core of calm, strength, and happiness.* Harmony/Rodale.

Hougaard, R., Carter, J., & Afton, M. (n.d.). *Connect with empathy, but lead with compassion.* Potential Project.

https://www.potentialproject.com/insights/connect-with-empathy-but-lead-with-compassion

Howe, N., & Strauss, W. (2024). *Generations: The history of America's future, 1584 to 2069 (Paperback)* William Morrow Paperbacks

Krznaric, R. (2015, June 4). *Empathy.* Penguin Books.

Leavitt, C. E. (2024). *Self-Awareness: An antidote to the rat race.* Psychology Today. https://www.psychologytoday.com/us/blog/sexual-mindfulness/202409/self-awareness-an-antidote-to-the-rat-race

LeBoeuf, R. (2022a, June 24). *A quote by Abraham Maslow.* Southern New Hampshire University. https://www.snhu.edu/about-us/newsroom/education/personal-growth-quotes

Lynch, M. (2022, February 11). *Intelligence quotient (IQ): How much does it matter.* The Edvocate. https://www.theedadvocate.org/intelligence-quotient-iq-how-much-does-it-matter/

Meyer, E. (n.d.). *The culture map: Breaking through the invisible boundaries of business.* Public Affairs.

Middleton, J. (2014). *Cultural intelligence: The competitive edge for leaders crossing boundaries.* Bloomsbury Publishing Plc.

Mindfulness meditation: How to do it. (2018, November 27). Mindful: Healthy Mind, Healthy Life. https://www.mindful.org/mindfulness-how-to-do-it/

Pérez-González, J.-C., Saklofske, D. H., & Mavroveli, S. (2020). Editorial: Trait emotional intelligence: Foundations, assessment, and education. *Frontiers in Psychology, 11.* https://doi.org/10.3389/fpsyg.2020.00608

A quote by Adam Grant. (2017). BrainyQuote. https://www.brainyquote.com/quotes/adam_grant_834184?src=t_emotional_intelligence

A quote by Alfred Adler. (2016, November 11). InspireMyKids. https://inspiremykids.com/great-empathy-quotes-kids-students-children/

A quote by Daniel Goleman. (2019). Goodreads.com. https://www.goodreads.com/work/quotes/587647-emotional-intelligence

A quote by Deborah Meaden. (2019). BrainyQuote. https://www.brainyquote.com/quotes/deborah_meaden_1037181?src=t_emotional_intelligence

A quote by Joseph B. Wirthlin. (2014). BrainyQuote. https://www.brainyquote.com/quotes/joseph_b_wirthlin_645942?src=t_self-control

A quote by Les Brown. (2024). Success. https://create.dibbly.com/d/Aq7VqqNNJiQSku9TUGKY

A quote by Marshall Goldsmith. (2018). BrainyQuote. https://www.brainyquote.com/quotes/marshall_goldsmith_899348?src=t_interpersonal

A quote by Neil Blumenthal. (2024). Brainyquote.com. https://www.brainyquote.com/quotes/neil_blumenthal_927656?src=t_emotional_intelligence

A quote by Paul Bloom. (2014). BrainyQuote. https://www.brainyquote.com/quotes/paul_bloom_644648?src=t_social

A quote by Travis Bradberry. (n.d.). BrainyQuote. https://www.brainyquote.com/quotes/travis_bradberry_734845?src=t_emotional_intelligence

A quote by William James. (2024). BrainyQuote. https://www.brainyquote.com/quotes/william_james_104186?src=t_generation

Raypole, C. (2020, November 13). *Emotional triggers: Definition and how to manage them.* Healthline. https://www.healthline.com/health/mental-health/emotional-triggers

Riess, H., Neporent, L., & Alsa, A. (2018). *The empathy effect: Seven neuroscience-based keys for transforming the way we live, love, work, and connect across differences.* Sounds True, Incorporated.

Ritter, S. M., Gu, X., Crijns, M., & Biekens, P. (2020). Fostering students' creative thinking skills by means of a one-year creativity training program. Students' Creative Thinking Skills. *PLOS ONE, 15*(3), e0229773. https://doi.org/10.1371/journal.pone.0229773

Salovey and Mayer's emotional intelligence. (2019, March 8). Exploring your mind. https://exploringyourmind.com/salovey-mayers-emotional-intelligence-theory/

Seladi-Schulman, J. (2018). *What part of the brain controls emotions? Fear, happiness, anger, love.* Healthline. https://www.healthline.com/health/what-part-of-the-brain-controls-emotions

Stanford-Binet Test. (2019). *Stanford-Binet Test.* Stanfordbinettest.com. https://stanfordbinettest.com/

Sutton, Ph.D., J. (2023, July 11). *30 Best Self-exploration questions, journal prompts, & tools.* Positive Psychology. https://positivepsychology.com/self-exploration/

Swift, C. (2023, April 11). *Goleman's 5 elements of EQ*. Accipio. https://www.accipio.com/eleadership/personal-effectiveness/golemans-5-elements-of-eq/

Tolle, E. (2004, August 19). *The Power of Now: A Guide to Spiritual Enlightenment*. New World Library

Tunnell, J. (2024, April 2). *20 Myths about emotional intelligence that might surprise you*. True You Journal. https://www.truity.com/blog/20-myths-about-emotional-intelligence-might-surprise-you

Yamada, R. (2023). *The impact of cross-cultural communication on organizational citizenship behavior in global virtual teams* (pp. 1–7) [Thesis]. Master Thesis Aalto University School of Business Management International. https://aaltodoc.aalto.fi/server/api/core/bitstreams/c80e10c3-03b1-42f8-9133-38963f52a310/content

Zaki, J. (2024). *The war for kindness*. Penguin Random House.

Printed in Great Britain
by Amazon